HOLY DAYS & HOLIDAYS

Volume II

Prayer Celebrations

with Children

Gaynell Bordes Cronin

1817

Harper & Row, Publishers, San Francisco

Cambridge, Hagerstown, New York, Philadelphia, Washington
London, Mexico City, São Paulo, Singapore, Sydney

Contents

Theme

New Year's Day	Peace blessing for seasons	John 1:1–4
Martin Luther King Day	Dream table/Gathering	Revelations 19–21
	Kingdom/Freedom	Galatians 3:26–29
Mardi Gras/Ash Wednesday	Celebration/Abstinence	Joel 2:12
Presidents' Day	Stars	Genesis 26:3–4
Earth Day	Creation/Garden Earth	Genesis 2:8–19
	Water/Caretaker/Care	Revelations 22:1–2
	Equinox	Luke 6:43–45
Palm Sunday	Blessing branches	
	Gospel drama	Matthew 21:1–11
April Fool's Day	Sendings	Numbers 22
	Being a Fool for Christ	
Good Friday	Remembering	John 19:17
		Psalm 31
May Day	Trees	Ezekiel 31:3–9
	Gift	Matthew 6:28–30
		Galatians 5:22–25, 6–8
Ascension Day	Baptism/Discipleship	
	Works of Love	
	Gospel drama	Matthew 28:16–29
Trinity Sunday	Oneness	John 17:20–22
	Creed/Profession of Faith	John 16:12–15
Midsummer's Eve	Sun/Solstice	
	John the Baptist	Psalm 19:1–6
Swithin's Day	Rain/Rainbow	
	Promise	Genesis (Noah Story)
Lammas Day	Bread/Eucharist	Luke 24:28–31
	God's Hands	1 Corinthians 10:16–17
Native Americans' Day	Land/Respect	
	Reverence/God's Care	
	Gospel drama	Mark 4:26–29
Harvest Day	Dwelling Place	Leviticus 23:1–43
	Gathering/Equinox	
	Harvest/Thanksgiving	
Columbus Day	Paths	Genesis 12:1–7
	Spirit	Genesis 28:10–15
	Journey	Tobit 5:17–22
World Peace Day	Seed	Isaiah 58:6–12
	Francis of Assisi	
St. Lucy's Day	Light/Solstice	1 Thessalonians 5:5–18

The Yule Wheel: A Symbol for All Seasons

One sign suggested for use through many of the prayer services is the Yule Wheel, reminiscent of the Advent Wreath. In medieval Europe it was a cross section cut from the Yule log at Christmas. Place it flat and divide it into four quarters representing the four seasons. On each segment place a candle, colored ribbon of that season, and a sign for the season (for example, winter, pine cone; spring, flower; summer, seashell; autumn, wheat sheaf). At the beginning of each season, light the season candle and pray for peace throughout the world during that season. If you cannot get a wheel from a log, simply make a round wreath or draw a log wheel. For additional information, see the Background Reflection for New Year's Day and the Prayer Celebration for a celebration of all the seasons.

The Yule Wheel

New Year's Day
Presidents' Day
Palm Sunday
Ascension Day
Midsummer's Eve
Native Americans' Day
World Peace Day
St. Lucy's Day

Blessings

Foreword

How do we learn to celebrate the "everydayness" of life?

That's the question that grounds this new volume of Gaynell Bordes Cronin's popular and prayerful *Holy Days and Holidays*. Gaynell's ability to break open the beauty hidden in the feasts and holidays we have celebrated for years makes this book a wonderful resource for families and parishes as they gather round their respective tables to discover and proclaim the presence of God among us.

The format of the book is very straightforward and easy to follow. After offering her readers a brief historical reflection on a particular holiday or holy day, Gaynell suggests a way to celebrate the event in our homes and concludes with a very understandable and simple prayer service. This format respects both the culture and original intent of the framers of the celebration as well as encourages readers to initiate celebrations in their homes. Best of all, it really works. Families everywhere have used previous editions of this work to introduce themselves to family ritual and prayer. While most of us are chary about being too formal or, God forbid, too long in our meal prayers and family gatherings, this book assures us of quality in a reasonable amount of time.

Gaynell Cronin's theology, as always, is impeccable. She exhibits a keen sense of what it means for God's people to be the church and develops prayers and rituals that help her readers to discover within themselves and their families everything that they need to pray authentically. Without ever being harsh, Gaynell reminds us that we often forget God's presence and power in our lives. At other times, we take it for granted. These beautifully designed prayer services help us to recapture what we sometimes forget or ignore.

There is another, perhaps even more important, value in this book. Because it so clearly demonstrates the depth of faith that is rooted in every culture in the world, it invites us to become cross cultural. A regular use of this book would make it impossible to maintain petty ethnic prejudices or forget the glory of God all over the world. By her choice of feasts and holidays that originate in so many diverse countries, Gaynell gently reminds us that God dwells among all the peoples of the world in ways we often forget, deny, or ignore. Children especially will benefit from this book's wise insights. By learning early about the customs and celebrations of many cultures, they will have a foundation for a growing appreciation of diversity in our churches and the world.

As a theologian, I cannot recommend this book too highly. Gaynell Bordes Cronin is a master at presenting complex truths in simple ways. Those who have used her work before will not be disappointed. Those who will experience her poetic gentleness for the first time will surely want to read and use her other works. *Holy Days and Holidays, Volume II* is a helpful, entertaining, and most of all prayerful book. Learning to pray about everyday things can only benefit us all.

Rev. John Rathschmidt, Ph.D.

Provincial Superior of the
Capuchin Franciscan Friars
of New York/New England

Introduction

Every Mardi Gras day, after the last carnival parade in New Orleans, we went to Grandma's house. I never knew what I enjoyed more, the parades or Grandma's homemade *beignets* (fried French doughnuts covered with powdered sugar). And regardless of your age, you were allowed to drink her chickory coffee with boiled milk. The smell and taste of the beignets and chickory still linger with me and the memory of gathering with aunts, uncles, and cousins awakens my feelings of what it means to belong and to be family.

We all have Grandmas in our lives. They are the people who provide a place for gathering, who welcome others with open hearts, who create an environment of belonging, who use the gifts of creation to celebrate God's presence, who make space sacred. And we are all invited to be Grandmas for others, to welcome and gather into our space all times and places—all the people of north, south, east, and west of long ago, today, and those yet to be.

And in making space sacred, we let it become a dwelling place for a journeying people—a place to give focus, a place to mark in ritual who we are, and who we are called to be. With gestures and signs, words and movements, we celebrate the seasons of our lives, the seasons of the natural world, the seasons of our hearts.

People have always, since ancient times, observed certain festivals at the turn of the seasons. Since each season reflects a different rhythm of the natural world, marking the beginning of the season has helped people become aware of what is happening within and around them. In this book, four colors have been chosen to represent the four seasons of the year —blue for winter, yellow for summer, green for spring, orange for autumn. It's a good idea to display a simple panel of cloth or other material in the chosen color during that season, in the room or area at school or home where you hold your prayer services. The changing panels for each season are visual reminders that we are a growing and journeying people seeking to be in touch with all the seasons of our lives.

Some churches display a season panel in their gathering place. On the panel is a sign for the day being celebrated during the coming week. Below the panel are placed copies of the prayer celebration or an excerpt from it. Families are invited to take these copies home for their own celebrations. At the beginning of each season, some churches provide a small piece of colored material of the season for families to bring home. A sense of oneness is nourished in knowing that others are marking in ritual in their home the same event as you are in your family.

Offering ritual for holy days and holidays helps us understand our history and our humanity. In ceremony we express our feelings about the changing seasons, the certainty of birth and death, our dreams and yearnings, our fears and joys—and we deepen our realization that all people of all places and times share this same human journey toward wholeness. We begin to realize how alike we are, the peoples of north, south, east, and west, and that the gifts of this planet Earth are for all—for us common people living with the common gifts of creation. While many names of these holy days and holidays reflect celebrations of the Western world, they have been designed to awaken within us our oneness as a people—humanity— and our responsibility to work for peace and justice in the whole world.

Since earliest recorded history, almost all celebrations of significant days and events were of a religious nature. In the Western world, they became known as "holy days." From these two words came the secular term *holiday.* This book offers twenty days and events to celebrate throughout the months and seasons of the year. A Background Reflection, Preparation, Project, Prayer Celebration are offered for each day. The Prayer Celebrations have been written for classes, families, or parishes. They center around four parts: Opening Greeting, a Reading, (an exchange specific to the day), and a Closing

Blessing. If the children are young, select only one or two parts of the four-part service. Copies of the Prayer Celebration are not necessary for the participants, because any response asked for will always first be given by the leader or reader. Since the Prayer Celebration of these holidays and holy days are grounded in scripture and themes, they can be used at other times during the year. For handy reference, themes and scripture have been noted in the front of the book. Location of specific blessings that you may want to use apart from the prayer service are also indicated. An explanation of the Yule Wheel, and where it is suggested for use, appears after the table of contents. There are clear directions for you as a leader, teacher, or parent before each of the prayer celebrations.

Gestures and signs, words and movement call not only for active involvement and participation in these celebrations, but speak to what we carry inside as a people and connect us to our past, present, and future. Through celebrations we get a glimpse into the mystery of God, the mystery of self, and the mystery of who we are as a people, and thus we are nourished for daily living. God is intimately present in all creation, dwelling within and among all of us. We simply need eyes that see and hearts that listen to recognize that presence. We need our deepest inside selves awakened and delighted through the celebration of that presence. And we need to do it together, as a one people of God, brothers and sisters in a gathered family.

Gaynell Bordes Cronin

New Year's Day

A Background Reflection

Down through the centuries, and even today, cultures and religions mark the beginning of a new year on different dates. Some countries celebrate the new year with the coming of spring; others with the first day of one of the seasons. Our Jewish brothers and sisters celebrate Rosh Hoshonah, the Jewish New Year, at the end of summer, close to the autumn equinox.

In medieval Europe most Christian countries considered New Year's Day to be on March 25. Our date of January 1 is inherited from the Romans when Julius Caesar, in honor of Janus, the god of all beginnings, changed the date from March to January. Janus was the god of two faces: one face looked back to the old year and the other looked forward. In Janus's right hand was a key that closed the gate of the old year and opened the new. In his left hand, a sceptor, symbol of power, waved over the heavens and the earth.

The intent of New Year's rites is to set aside the past and welcome a rebirth of time. The beginning of a new year heralds creation beginning anew as we enter another cycle of time and are reborn in the spirit of God. Since the yearning for a new beginning is so deep within all people, the new year festival was often the most important holiday of the year. For some people, it was a day of merriment, for others, an occasion of seriousness and prayer.

Seen as a day of merriment, New Year is a noisy time with sirens, whistles, bells, and party horns. This din, according to ancient customs, chases away the forces of darkness. Resolutions to "turning over a new leaf" are made. Apples dipped in honey are eaten as a sign of promising a new direction in life. And it is said that if you think positively and are as happy as possible when the New Year arrives, you will be rewarded with a year of good health, wealth, and happiness.

Open house is extended to remember old friends and make new ones. Wishes for happiness in the new year are toasted and hearty handshakes exchanged. Football bowl games and parades are popular throughout the United States on this day. Many families reach deep into their heritage by eating certain foods to ensure luck for the New Year; for example, the French may eat pancakes; Germans may eat fish; and the Swiss, whipped cream. In some homes, black-eyed peas are ceremoniously eaten. Since food ritualizes and expresses deep beliefs one has as family, it is good to continue or introduce a food that represents your own family heritage.

As an occasion for prayer, some denominations have informal gatherings for a quiet time to meditate on the New Year. Many people consider it a good time to heal disputes and ask forgiveness for any wrongs they have committed or hurts inflicted on others during the past year. Some countries designate this day as one of universal brotherhood and sisterhood, while some religions pray for the gift of peace throughout the earth in the name of Jesus, the Prince of Peace, and in honoring Mary as Queen of Peace.

As with other celebrations, fire and light play an important role in worship and in marking new beginnings from the ancient Egyptians down to our present age. From the Yule log, fire was kindled and a blessing made for each coming season of the year. A round cross section was cut from a felled tree. Round and turning like a wheel, this section was marked into four segments representing the four seasons. The calendar-like wheel was called a Yule, and the tree log from which it was cut was the Yule log. As each season of the year came, a fire was kindled and the Yule log placed in it while the separate Yule wheel was turned as the people prayed that their God be kind to them and the earth during that season.

Let us join other men and women as they pray the Hebrew blessing of Aaron to the people and ask God's spirit to come and rest on the people and the land in peace:

> The Lord bless you and keep you.
> The Lord's face shine on you and be
> gracious to you.
> The Lord look kindly on you and
> give you peace.

Numbers 6:24–26 (adapted)

Preparations

directions

Hang the blue panel for the season of winter. Place the Yule Wheel before the panel.

Choose five readers for the blessing that appears at the end of the celebration.

Alert participants of the blessing they will give as they turn in the four directions of the earth.

Ask participants to think of ways they will share their goodness during the coming year. Each way is recorded on pieces of paper, in words or in signs. Place these pieces around the Yule Wheel during the celebration.

materials

Yule Wheel
Four candles
Paper and pencils
Blue panel for winter

Project

Cut a Yule Wheel from wood or make one from cardboard or styrofoam. (An Advent wreath could also be used.)

Place four candles on the Wheel. Decorate each candle to represent one season of the year. You may also want to add colored ribbons that correspond to the four banners or panels used throughout the year: blue (winter), green (spring), yellow (summer), orange (fall).

Prayer Celebration

Opening Greeting

LEADER: In gathering as the people of God, we find in each other the hope and joy of a new beginning. Quietly in our hearts we remember one good thing that happened to us during this past year,

(pause)

and we say, "Thank you, Lord."

ALL: Thank You, Lord.

LEADER: In our hearts, we recall one person who journeyed with us through the good and not so good times,

(pause)

and we say, "Thank you, Lord."

ALL: Thank you, Lord.

LEADER: In our oneness, we ask forgiveness of anyone we may have hurt by offering a sign of peace,

(pause)

and we say, "Thank you, Lord."

ALL: Thank you, Lord.

Blessing of the Seasons for Peace

LEADER: Lord, bless us throughout all seasons with joy. Bless this our Yule Wheel. The fire kindled on our Yule becomes a sign of your light and blessing for all the seasons of our heart.

READER 1: We kindle this light for spring.

(candle lighted)

May each spring shower bring new life, your life to the land, Lord. May gentle rains fall and renew our hearts with hope for a new world. And throughout this spring season of the year, let there be peace, your peace, Lord, on earth.

ALL: Let there be peace, your peace, Lord, on earth.

READER 2: We kindle this light for summer.

(candle lighted)

May the bright sun of summer warm the earth for the blooming of flowers and the growing of trees and plants. May the sun's rays give strength and health to our bodies and enlighten our minds. And throughout this summer season of the year, let there be peace, your peace, Lord, on earth.

ALL: Let there be peace, your peace, Lord, on earth.

READER 3: We kindle this light for fall.

(candle lighted)

May the harvest yield the fruit of the land and give food to the hungry. May each leaf that falls be a sign of happiness for all. And throughout this fall season of the year, let there be peace, your peace, Lord, on earth.

ALL: **Let there be peace, your peace, Lord, on earth.**

READER 4: **We kindle this light for winter.**

(candle lighted)

May the winter wind blow goodwill into our hearts. May the crisp, fresh air fill our lives with friendship for all people as our brothers and sisters. And throughout this winter season of the year, let there be peace, your peace, Lord, on earth.

ALL: **Let there be peace, your peace, Lord, on earth.**

LEADER: **Jesus is the same yesterday, today, and forever— through all seasons and all places. We turn to the four corners of our earth to send God's blessing of peace for this year of 19_____.
To the east: May you live in peace.**

ALL: **May you live in peace.** (Sign of cross is made to the east.)

LEADER: **To the south: May you live in peace.**

ALL: **May you live in peace.** (Sign of cross is made to the south.)

LEADER: **To the west: May you live in peace.**

ALL: **May you live in peace.** (Sign of cross is made to the west).

LEADER: **To the north: May you live in peace.**

ALL: **May you live in peace.** (Sign of the cross is made to the north.)

LEADER: **And to each of us gathered for a new beginning, a new year: May you live in peace.**

ALL: **May you live in peace.** (People greet each other with these words.)

A Reading

LEADER: **The Bible begins with the words "In the beginning, God created the universe." And in this beginning creation becomes gift from God, the gift giver. We listen to the words of John to discover Jesus, the Word, as gift from the beginning for all of us.**

READER 5: **"In the beginning was the Word, and the Word was with God, and the Word was God. He was in the beginning with God; all things were made through him, and without him not one thing was made in all creation. In him was life, and the life was the light to all people."**

John 1:1–4 (adapted)

This is the Word of the Lord.

ALL: **Thanks be to God.**

"Ringing Out the Old Year" Litany

LEADER: "Ring out the old, ring in the new,
Ring happy bells across the snow
The year is going, let it go.
Ring out the false, ring in the true.
Because God made all
  beginnings,
together we can say,

ALL: Ring out the old, ring in the new!

LEADER: Ring out the feud of rich and poor
Ring out the want, the hurt,
  the sad.
The faithless coldness of the times
  no more.
Because the Word is our source of
  life, together we can say,

ALL: Ring out the old, ring in the new!

LEADER: Ring out the thousand wars of old
Ring in the thousand years of peace
Ring in the love of truth and right
Let the common law of good be told.
Because the Word is the Prince
of Peace, together we can say,

ALL: Ring out the old, ring in the new!

LEADER: Ring in the valiant, true, and free
The largest heart, the kindest hand.
Ring out the darkness of the land.
Ring in the Christ that is to be.
Because the Word brought light
to all people, together we can say,

ALL: Ring out the old, ring in the new!

Alfred, Lord Tennyson *Ringing Out of the
Old Year,* (adapted)

LEADER: Christ is yesterday, today, and
tomorrow and so we say,
Through him, with him, in him,
in the unity of the Holy Spirit,
all glory and honor is yours,
almighty Father, forever and ever.

ALL: Amen.

LEADER: On your Yule Wheel we place a
sign of the good we will try to
live and bring to others, during
all seasons of the year, from east
to west, from north to south.

(Signs are placed around Yule
Wheel.)

Closing Blessing

LEADER: Bow your head for God's
blessing as you live peace
throughout the land.
The Lord bless you and keep
you.

ALL: Amen.

LEADER: The Lord's face shine on you and
be gracious.

ALL: Amen.

LEADER: The Lord look kindly on you and
give you peace.

ALL: Amen.

LEADER: May God the creator, the Son
the redeemer, and the Spirit the
life giver, be with you forever.

ALL: Amen.

Martin Luther King Day

A Background Reflection

Only four people in U.S. history have been honored with national holidays: Christopher Columbus, George Washington, Abraham Lincoln, and now civil rights leader Martin Luther King, Jr. The Federal Holiday Commission in 1986 honored the birth of King on January 20 by asking Americans to pledge themselves to make the world a place where equality and justice, freedom and peace would grow and flourish. People were asked to commit themselves to living the dream by

> Loving, not hating,
> Showing understanding, not anger,
> Making peace, not war.

This twentieth day of January can become a time for rededicating ourselves to the goal of equal rights for all Americans and a day to honor the most famous southerner of our twentieth century.

But who is this man who cherished racial and religious diversity, who saw the civil rights revolution not as a black rebellion but as a covenant of white and black, Christian and Jews, standing together for decency. A winner of the Nobel Peace Prize, King was deeply influenced by the teachings of Mohandas Gandhi (the famous civil rights leader in India) and was committed to nonviolence in his pursuit of social justice for black Americans.

Who is this man called by some the "conscience of the nation" and by others the "apostle of nonviolence"? Many people speak of a profound bond of mutual respect, and a deep sense of solidarity with the mission of King. Perhaps they feel thus because King's goal was not only justice for America's blacks but human rights for all people and peace everywhere. His challenge to us is to share a vision of a compassionate and open society.

The son of a pastor and a school teacher, King grew up in Atlanta, Georgia, and was ordained a Baptist minister. While serving as a pastor in Montgomery, Alabama, he led a bus boycott that lasted more than a year but ended in the desegregation of buses. Rosa Parks, a black seamstress who refused to relinquish her seat to a white man, triggered this bus boycott. Of Parks, King later wrote, "She was anchored to that seat by the accumulated indignities of days gone by and the boundless aspirations of generations yet unborn."

After this successful bus boycott, King and his followers saw the need for similar efforts throughout the South. Together, they organized the Southern Christian Leadership Conference (SCLC) and struggled throughout the late 1950s and 1960s to end segregation and racism in the United States. In Birmingham, Alabama, King led mass demonstrations to protest segregation of public facilities. Here he was arrested and while in solitary confinement wrote his famous "Letter from the Birmingham Jail," which set forth his theory of nonviolent civil disobedience.

Throughout his life King's philosophy remained the same: to meet the forces of hate with the power of love, to forgive your enemies, and to use no violence. Even though he, his family, and the entire civil rights movement was increasingly plagued by violence, King never lost his faith in nonviolence or in the essential decency of people, black and white. Climaxing in the historic march on Washington in August 1963, King addressed 250,000 demonstrators gathered at the Lincoln Memorial in a speech that came to epitomize the man and his struggle:

> Even though we face the difficulties of today and tomorrow, I still have a dream. I have a dream that one day this nation will rise up and live out the true meaning of its creed, "we hold these truths to be self-evident, that all people are created equal."

As with all men and women who deepen their understanding of what it is to be brothers and sisters made in the image and likeness of God, King's compassion for the victims of prejudice extended to poor people so that they too could claim their share of the American promise. He also spoke out against the war in Vietnam because he believed that peace and freedom could not be separated.

While in Memphis, Tennessee, supporting sanitation workers who were striking for better wages and working conditions, King was murdered by an assassin's bullet. The day before his funeral, his wife, Coretta Scott King, after leading a silent memorial march with her three oldest children through Memphis, addressed the crowd at City Hall with these words:

> We must carry on because this is the way he would have wanted it to have been. We are going to continue his work to make all people truly free and to make every person feel that he or she is a human being.

Like Martin Luther King, Jr., we are challenged to share in the life of the poor and oppressed as we work for social justice and as we deepen our understanding through the words of Paul in Scripture that we are all children of God, we are one.

> So God does not see you as Jew or Greek. God does not see you as slave or free. God does not see you as man or woman. There are no differences among you. You are all one in Jesus.

Galatians 3:26–28 (adapted)

Preparations

directions

Use the blue panel (for winter) as a cloth to spread on a gathering table. Place the project words "Our Dream" down the middle of the table. Distribute placemats around the table.

Place a candle to represent the Dream Candle of Peace on the table.

Choose six readers.

Alert participants that they will be sharing the symbol they have made on their placemats.

materials

Candle
Colored paper
Scissors and crayons/magic markers
A table

Project

Make the words "Our Dream" for the center of the table (draw, paint, cut out, or so on).

Cut out 11 × 18-inch placemats from colored construction paper. Participants decorate their placemats with their names, symbols of the work they do, and their dreams of who we are and what we can be as a people.

Prayer Celebration

Opening Greeting

LEADER: Welcome to a day of celebration, a day of remembering the dreams of Martin Luther King, Jr., a day of pledging ourselves to loving, not hating; showing understanding, not anger; making peace, not war. Lord, we are your people. You have made each of us in your own image and likeness. As we light our Dream Candle of Peace, we ask for hands and hearts that will help build a world where equality and justice, freedom and peace, will grow and flourish.

The peace of the Lord be with you.

ALL: And also with you.

The Readings

LEADER: Paul had a dream in which all people could live together as one. It is through Jesus that we know how deeply God loves all of us. This is what Paul told the people of Galatia.

READER 1: "Now that you have put your trust in Jesus, you are children of God. God does not see you as Jew or Greek. God does not see you as a slave or a free person. God does not see you as a man or a woman. There are no differences among you. You are all one in Jesus. If you belong to Jesus, you are truly children of Abraham our Father. What was promised Abraham, God will give to you, too."

Galatians 3:26–29 (adapted)

This is the Word of the Lord.

ALL: Thanks be to God.

LEADER: Martin Luther King, Jr., had that same dream as Paul. One day at the Lincoln Memorial in Washington, D.C., he spoke of this dream to all of us.

READER 2: "I say to you today, my friends, even though we face the difficulties of today and tomorrow, I still have a dream. It is a dream deeply rooted in the American dream. I have a dream that one day this nation will rise up and live out the true meaning of its creed: 'We hold these truths to be self-evident, that all people are created equal.'"

LEADER: What is the one difficulty that you face today?

(pause)

What self-evident truth is part of your creed?

READER 3: "I have a dream that one day on the red hills of Georgia the sons and daughters of former slaves and the sons and daughters of former slaveowners will be able to sit down together at the table of brotherhood and sisterhood. I have a dream that my four little children will one day live in a nation where they will not be judged by the color of their skin, but by the content of their character."

LEADER: Whom would you find difficult to invite to sit down at your table?

(pause)

How do you feel when you are judged by others? How do you judge others?

(pause)

READER 4: "I have a dream that one day every valley shall be exalted, every hill and mountain shall be made low, the rough places will be made plain, and the crooked places will be made straight, and the glory of the Lord shall be revealed, and all flesh shall see it together."

LEADER: What rough places are you making smooth?

(pause)

What crooked places are you making straight?

(pause)

READER 5: "When we allow freedom to ring — when we let it ring from every city and every hamlet, from every state and every city, we will be able to speed up that day when all of God's children, black and white, Jews and Gentiles, Protestants and Catholics, will be able to join hands and sing in the words of the old spiritual, 'Free at last, Free at last, Great God Almighty, we are free at last!'"

LEADER: What keeps you in your own kind of slavery?

(pause)

Who helps you to become free?

(pause)

The Freedom Litany

LEADER: People have spoken of freedom down through the centuries. They lived their lives with the dream of one day gathering together as one in the name of God. We give thanks for these dream makers and dream keepers. For Moses, who brought a people across the desert from slavery to freedom, so that one day we will say together, "Free at last, free at last!"

ALL: Free at last, free at last!

LEADER: For prophets Isaiah and John the Baptist who helped the people remember the dream so that one day we will say together, "Free at last, free at last!"

ALL: Free at last, free at last!

LEADER: For Mary who taught Jesus the dreams of his people so that one day we will say together, "Free at last, free at last!"

ALL: Free at last, free at last!

LEADER: For Frederick Douglass, who wrote and spoke against slavery, so that one day we will say together, "Free at last, free at last!"

ALL: Free at last, free at last!

LEADER: For Harriet Tubman, who helped escaped slaves reach freedom through the underground railroads, so that one day we will say together, 'Free at last, free at last!'

ALL: Free at last, free at last!

LEADER: For Mary McLeod Bethune, who founded a college to help improve social and educational opportunities for blacks, so that one day we will say together, "Free at last, free at last!"

ALL: Free at last, free at last!

LEADER: For Rosa Parks, a black seamstress who refused to give her bus seat to a white person, so that one day we will say together, "Free at last, free at last!"

ALL: Free at last, free at last!

LEADER: For Martin Luther King, Jr., a Baptist minister who struggled for the rights of black people and the poor to share in the promise of America, so that one day we will say together, "Free at last, free at last!"

ALL: Free at last, free at last!

LEADER: For each of us who strive for the recognition of human rights for all people around the planet Earth, so that one day we will say together, "Free at last, free at last!"

ALL: Free at last, free at last!

LEADER: Lord, we thank you for these people who awaken us to the needs of others and to the call to work for peace and justice in our world so that one day we will join hands before you, our God, and say,
"Free at last, free at last.
Great God Almighty, in your love, we are free at last!"

The Table Gathering

LEADER: Because the spirit of God lives in us, we each give vision and shape to the dream of one people living in justice and peace. We gather before our table of brotherhood and sisterhood on which we have placed who we are through what we dream.

(pause for gathering)

To the banquet table of the Lord we have all been invited. We recognize this call through a reading from the Book of Revelations.

READER 6: "I saw an angel standing on the sun and shouting in a loud voice, 'Come and gather together for God's great feast.' Then I heard the sound of a voice saying, 'Praise God all people both great and small. Let us rejoice and be glad, let us give praise for God's greatness. Happy are those who have been invited to the wedding feast.' Then I saw a new heaven and a new earth. And a loud voice spoke again: 'Now God's home is with all people. God lives with them and they are God's people. All tears have been wiped from their eyes. And there is no more death, no more grief or crying or pain. Come and gather together at the table for God's great feast.'"

Revelations 19:17, 5, 9, 21:1–4 (adapted)

LEADER: As we wait this day, we speak of who we are through the work we do and the dreams we share.

(Participants talk about and explain their placemats.)

As we yearn for this banquet day, as we work to make this old world into a new one, as we help one another live the dream, let us join hands and say together the prayer of the promised and dreamed-for kingdom of God.

ALL: Our Father who art in heaven, hallowed be your name; your kingdom come; your will be done on earth as it is in heaven. Give us this day our daily bread; and forgive us our trespasses as we forgive those who trespass against us; and lead us not into temptation, but deliver us from evil. Amen.

Mardi Gras/Ash Wednesday

A Background Reflection

There are rhythms to life—in the four seasons, in day and night, in the beating of our hearts, in breathing in and out. We live opposites daily through beginnings and endings, goodbyes and hellos, waitings and fulfillings. The yearning of the heart reflects itself in apparent contradictions—wanting to celebrate and to abstain, to rejoice and to mourn. Ecclesiastes captures this spirit rhythm in which we live by announcing that there is a "time for everything." The celebration of Mardi Gras and the immediate entry into Lent with Ash Wednesday offers us an experience of opposites—of celebrating and abstaining.

Carnival time, a time of feasting, revelery, and gaiety, which culminates on Mardi Gras day, actually begins on Twelfth Night (the twelfth night after Christmas). During the following weeks, parades and masked balls are held. When I was in New Orleans, it was the custom for young people to gather weekly for King Cake parties. A bean was baked into a specially made round cake with the carnival colors of purple, green, and gold. Whoever got the bean was king or queen for the evening and had the party at his or her home the following week. This continued until Mardi Gras.

On the Tuesday before Ash Wednesday, Mardi Gras day, people gather in the streets dressed in costume to watch parades of gaily and elaborately decorated floats from which people throw favors and trinkets. The best-known carnival celebrations are centered in New Orleans, the Caribbean Islands, Trinidad, Rio de Janeiro, and parts of France.

These carnival celebrations encourage a sense of make-believe, with people masking themselves and wearing costumes. For an entire day, one can pretend to be someone else, can play a role. Like the child or the actor, we are invited to play "let's pretend." Actually, in earlier times people wore these masks to scare away the demons who were thought to spread the darkness of winter.

The French name Mardi Gras means Fat Tuesday. It was the custom on this day to eat as much fat as possible before the rigid abstinence from all these foods during the forty days of Lent. Pancakes were eaten in England, while in France and Germany, doughnuts fried in deep fat were the ritual food. Even the leader of Mardi Gras parades who rides a float with a huge ox, and the gaily costumed butchers who throw sweets and trinkets, are there to remind us of what we are soon to be without.

On Ash Wednesday morning, the debris of Mardi Gras lies in the streets, in sharp contrast to the people who are walking home from church with a smear of ashes (from the burning of previous year's blessed palms) on their foreheads as they begin the journey of Lent. For all Christian churches, Lent is a forty-day period of preparation that ends in Holy Week and builds to the joyous celebration of Easter. This is a time of increased penance, prayer, service to others, and almsgiving. It is the traditional time to pay increased attention to God in your life.

Sprinkling your head with ashes is an ancient sign of repentence we have accepted from Jewish tradition. Jonah (3:5–9), Jeremiah (6:26, 25:3), and Matthew (11:21) all show that wearing ashes was a sign of penance and sorrow. The Christian custom of marking the head with ashes began during the papacy of Gregory the Great (6th century A.D.), when public penitents came barefoot to the church to perform penances for wrongdoing. In recognition that no one is free from sin and wanting to stand by these penitents, friends and relatives began to come. Soon ashes were given to the entire gathered assembly. Many Christian denominations today observe Ash Wednesday with the distribution of ashes.

Preparations

directions

Choose three areas for each of the three stations.

At the first station, gather with noisemakers and masks.

At the second station hang streamers.

At the third station hang the blue panel with a cross for the season of winter and place before it a purple-covered box or chest (to use for burying the streamers during the ceremony).

Also place here pencils and papers and a container for burning, such as a metal plate or pan.

Make masks.

Make streamers.

Choose two readers.

Gather noisemakers (a drum, a hand bell, tambourines, and so forth). These will be used at Station One, for one of the litany prayers, and to mark the transition from Mardi Gras to Ash Wednesday.

Be prepared to call each participant by name—write a list, or provide name tags.

Explain to participants that during the ceremony they will be writing on small pieces of paper, which will then be burned. Explain the significance of burning one's Lenten promise. (Like smoke, our spirits lift in knowing we can do all things in Jesus.)

Teach participants the version of "When the Saints Go Marching In" used in the service.

Choose appropriate music if you wish to use it during the distribution of the ashes from the burned Lenten promises.

materials

Winter panel (blue)
Small scraps of paper
Pencils
Metal plate for burning
Noisemakers
Purple, gold, green crepe paper
Scissors and crayons
Box
Purple cloth or paper

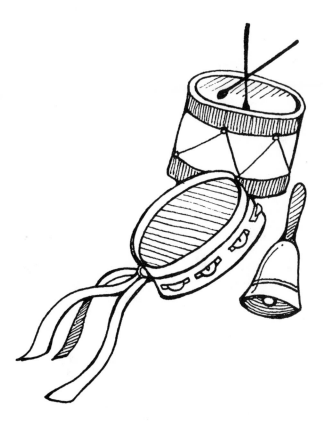

Project

Make long streamers from the crepe paper (the carnival colors are purple, gold, and green). Cut 1-inch × 6-foot strips. With felt-tip markers or white paper, write or cut out letters or words expressing the carnival season, such as Joy, Happy, Hope, Wow, Alleluia. (Make sure that Alleluia is included.) Place words on streamers.

Make masks.

With purple cloth or paper, make a large cross, and pin it to the winter panel.

Prayer Celebration

Opening Greeting

LEADER: It is said that there is a time for everything, a time to celebrate and to abstain, a time to rejoice and to mourn. We come together to mark the days of opposites, Mardi Gras and Ash Wednesday.

At First Station

LEADER: In the spirit of the Carnival season, we gather with music, song, movement, and hearts of joy to celebrate Mardi Gras. We wear masks and enter into a world of make-believe and pretend.

(Masks are put on.)

With our noisemakers we tell the world of our joy in being able to celebrate life.

(noisemakers)

And through movement and song we sing,
(to the tune of "When the Saints Go Marching In")
O, when the sun begins to shine
O, when the sun begins to shine
O, Lord, I want to be in that number
When the sun begins to shine

When our hearts show out their love,

(Sing while marching around.)

At Second Station

LEADER: We gather before our carnival streamers, which tell of our joy before the Lord as we speak our praise, our Alleluia.

READER 1: Lord, from where we have come and to where we are going, we say, "Amen. Praise God. Alleluia."

ALL: Amen. Praise God. Alleluia.

(Music makers play during response.)

READER 1: For beginnings, middles, and ends and all the moments of being alive, we say, "Amen, Praise God, Alleluia."

ALL: Amen. Praise God. Alleluia.

(Music makers play.)

READER 1: For faith to believe in mystery, we say, "Amen, Praise God. Alleluia."

ALL: Amen. Praise God. Alleluia.

(Music makers play.)

READER 1: For hope that opens us to surprise, we say, "Amen. Praise God. Alleluia."

(Music makers play.)

For love that gives us grateful hearts, we say, "Amen, Praise God. Alleluia."

ALL: Amen. Praise God. Alleluia.

(Music makers play.)

READER 1: Through God and with God, in the unity of the spirit, all honor and glory is yours, world without end.

ALL: Amen.

(Bell or drum slowly intones to count of twelve as everyone becomes silent and takes off masks. As they move to Third Station, they take pencil and paper from box.)

At Third Station

LEADER: We begin the season of Lent as we stand before the cross, a sign of our forty-day journey toward Easter. This is our time to pay attention to God in our life through prayer, penance, and doing acts of loving-kindness to others.

Write on your paper one thing that you promise to do this Lent to become more aware of God in yourself and others.

(pause)

As I call you by name, come forward and place your folded paper in the plate in front of the cross.

(calling of names)

We gather these offerings and light them. As we watch them burn, we deepen our promises in our heart. As the smoke lifts, so do our spirits in knowing that we can do all things in Jesus who lives in us and among us.

(lighting and burning)

A Reading

LEADER: In this reading from Joel, we reflect on the call to turn to God with all our heart for God is tender and compassionate.

READER 2: "Yet even now, says the Lord, return to me with all your heart, with fasting, with weeping, and with mourning; and rend your hearts and not your garments. Return to the Lord, your God, for God is gracious and merciful, slow to anger, and abounding in steadfast love."

Joel 2:12–13

This is the Word of the Lord.

ALL: Thanks be to God.

LEADER: Now take a moment to think of the ways you can turn to God with all your heart.

Blessing and Giving of Ashes

LEADER: We extend our hands over the ashes in blessing. Lord, Bless these ashes, which we use as a sign that we have turned to you with all our heart. Pardon our wrongdoings. Keep us faithful to our Lenten promises.

(Leader marks the forehead of each person with the ashes while saying:)

"Keep Lent and turn to God with all your heart."

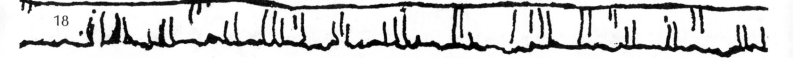

The Alleluia Farewell

LEADER: Our days are now different. The Alleluia, our acclamation of cheer, will not be spoken or sung during Lent.

In ceremony, we take down our streamers and place them in our Lenten box.

(pause)

On Easter, we will lift them from this darkened place, and in the new light of the resurrection display and proclaim the Alleluia of our Risen Lord.

Let us bow our heads for God's blessing.

Come back to the Lord with all your heart.

ALL: Amen.

LEADER: Leave the past in ashes.

ALL: Amen.

LEADER: Turn to God with prayers and fasting.

ALL: Amen.

LEADER: For God is tender and compassionate.

ALL: Amen.

LEADER: In silence and quiet, let us go forth to love and serve the Lord through the way we live our Lenten promises.

ALL: In the name of the Father, and of the Son, and of the Holy Spirit, Amen.

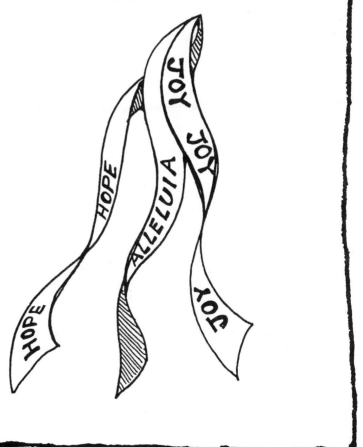

Presidents' Day

A Background Reflection

Although the lives of George Washington and Abraham Lincoln were dramatically different, they shared similar ideals and aspirations. Both men believed in a government of and by the people. Through the War of Independence, Washington became convinced that "United we stand, divided we fall." Likewise after the Civil War, Lincoln urged the people to finish binding up the nation's wounds so that we could be one.

Lincoln, born in a simple log cabin, was a self-educated man who read the Bible, Shakespeare, Aesop's Fables, the classics, and any law books he could find. First a clerk in a general store, then postmaster, general surveyor, and finally lawyer and member of the state legislature, Lincoln remained relatively unknown at age 40. However, while running for the senatorial election against Stephen Douglas, Lincoln came into national prominence through their debates where he showed an exceptional knowledge of U.S. history and government, genius as an orator, and analytical skill. Through these debates Lincoln expressed his deep conviction that slavery must be abolished. On the hundredth anniversary of Lincoln's birth, black leader Booker T. Washington spoke of Abraham Lincoln's *Emancipation Proclamation*, which formally gave black slaves their freedom, and he quoted Lincoln: "As I would not be a slave, so I would not be a master."

Lincoln was a peace-loving man. In his second Inaugural Address, Lincoln urged reconciliation between North and South following the Civil War: "With malice toward none and charity for all." The poet Carl Sandberg commemorated Lincoln with these words: "A man...both steel and velvet...hard as rock and soft as drifting fog." The Lincoln Memorial stands in Washington, D.C., as a tribute to this President.

Like Lincoln, George Washington, our first president and "father of the country," was a folk hero. Like a knight in shining armor for the nation, he led the people in gaining freedom from England and helped establish our constitution with a government by the people. His life reflects high ideals of government courage as a soldier, patience as a commander, and faithful devotion to his country.

Another founding father, Thomas Jefferson, said of Washington, "His mind was powerful and penetration strong, judgment sound—he was little aided by invention or imagination but sure in conclusion—prudent with his justice inflexible, and we place him in the same constellation that merits remembrance." Washington is considered a great statesman whose birthday was celebrated throughout the nation even before his death. Later stories have capitalized on the legends of Washington cutting down the cherry tree, throwing a silver dollar across the Potomac River, and his professed inability to tell a lie.

In honor of his birthday on February 22, Washington's farewell address is read each year in the U.S. Senate. The Washington Monument, in the shape of an Egyptian obelisk, the main memorial dedicated to him, stands in Washington, D.C. There are no prescribed ways to celebrate this day but Washington Birthday sales with merchants serving cherry pie have become increasingly popular. In a few states, the joint celebration of Washington's and Lincoln's birthday is known as Presidents' Day. Local stores sometimes hold special sales.

The week of Washington's birthday, called Brotherhood Week, is sponsored by the National Conference of Christians and Jews to bring about greater understanding between different religions and races. George Washington stands as their symbol of trying to free the nation of religious and racial discrimination and in ensuring that all Americans are treated equally as citizens of this democracy and as brothers and sisters in one common family. Washington once assured the people that the privilege of worshiping God in any way they wished was both a choice blessing and a precious gift.

Wreath laying ceremonies for both of these presidents occur on their birthdays: February 11 for Abraham Lincoln and February 22 for George Washington. Wreaths laid on a sacred venerated object denote glory, victory, or dedication. Laurel wreaths were awarded to victors of Olympic games, wreaths of roses were worn by Roman emperors, olive wreaths were given to those of literary merit, grass wreaths recognized heroes and heroines, and wreaths made of oak leaves became a reward for saving a life. We honor with an oak wreath Washington and Lincoln, and all men and women who by their presence work to build the earth in peace and justice for all.

Long ago, God promised Abraham that his descendants would be as numerous as the stars in the sky. As we build this earth together, we discover that every nation has its own stars, its own founders and builders who give vision and hope to the people. We continue to have them in our life today. They are men and women like Abraham and Sarah, Isaac and Rebecca, who were not afraid to take new journeys with the faith and conviction that we can still live as a one people. These stars blaze new paths of understanding and give new light to what it is to live in freedom.

Because the six-pointed star, the Star of David, is used in the Prayer Service, it is interesting to note that each point of the star represents an attribute of God: power, wisdom, majesty, love, mercy, justice. In living these qualities, men and women image God to others.

Preparations

directions

Hang the blue panel for the season of winter. (If you have a Yule Wheel, you may want to place it before the panel for your oak wreath to rest on.)

Choose participants to place an oak wreath before the panel and stars for Lincoln and Washington on the panel.

Participants hold their name star. Remind them that as they are called by name to put their name star on the panel, they are asked to name aloud the quality they have chosen in living for others.

Be prepared to call each participant by name.

Have a punch bowl of a favorite beverage, with cups for each participant already filled set around bowl.

materials

Blue panel
Colored paper for stars and oak leaves
Crayons/magic markers
Scissors
Pins
Bowl and cups
Favorite beverage

Project

Make a wreath of oak leaves.

Participants make and place their names on cut-out six-pointed stars. They choose and write one of the six qualities of God: power, wisdom, majesty, love, mercy, justice.

Make two larger stars. Write the names of Abraham Lincoln and George Washington on them.

Prayer Celebration

Opening Greeting

LEADER: We gather to celebrate the vision and hope of all men and women who work for peace and justice in a government of the people, by the people, and for the people. With George Washington and Abraham Lincoln, we continue to preserve a land of freedom that welcomes and affirms the message on our Statue of Liberty:

> Give me your tired, your poor,
> Your huddled masses
> yearning to breathe free,
> The wretched refuse of
> your teeming shore.
> Send these, the homeless,
> tempest-tost to me.
> I lift my lamp beside the
> golden door."

Emma Lazarus

In celebration of the birthdays of Washington and Lincoln, we place this oak wreath before our banner, a symbol of honor and gratitude for preserving the rights of the people.

(pause)

The Words of our Presidents

LEADER: Washington's Farewell Address is read each year on his birthday in the U.S. Senate. We listen to the words of our first president, who helped establish our Constitution and lived a life in faithful devotion to his country.

READER 1: "Observe good faith and justice toward all nations. Cultivate peace and harmony with all. Let religion and morality enjoin this conduct as well as good policy . . . As I leave office, I anticipate the sweet enjoyment of partaking in the influence of good laws under a free government, the ever favorite object of my heart, and the happy reward of our mutual cares, labors, and dangers."

Washington's Farewell Address, 1796 (adapted)

LEADER: On our banner we place a star for George Washington.

(pause)

We listen to the words of Abraham Lincoln, our sixteenth president of the United States, as he urges reconciliation between the North and South following the Civil War.

READER 2: "With malice toward none; with charity for all; with firmness in the right, as God gives us to see the right, let us strive on to finish the work we are in; to bind up the nation's wounds; to care for those who borne the battle, and for widows, and orphans—to do all which may achieve and cherish a just and lasting peace among ourselves, and with all nations."

Lincoln's Second Inaugural Address, 1865

LEADER: On our banner we place a star for Abraham Lincoln

(pause)

The Star Litany

LEADER: Every nation has its own stars, its own founders and builders who give vision and hope to the people. They are people of faith who believe that we can one day live as a one people. We listen to the words of God spoken to Isaac and Rebecca in the Book of Genesis.

READER 3: "Live here, and I will be with you and bless you. I am going to give all this territory to you and your descendants. I will keep the promise I made to your father Abraham. I will give you as many descendants as there are stars in the sky. All the nations will ask me to bless them as I have blessed your descendants."

Genesis 26:3–4 GNB

This is the Word of the Lord.

ALL: Thanks be to God.

LEADER: We are the descendants of Abraham and Sarah, Isaac and Rebecca, Jacob and Rachel. We are shining stars when we live in peace and justice with all people. As your name is called please come forward. As you place your name star on the banner, name aloud your chosen quality as a sign of the particular way you will try to live as God's light for all the people.

(pause for calling of names and presenting of stars)

We remember that each of our stars is the six-pointed Star of David. Each point represents a different attribute of God: power, wisdom, majesty, love, mercy, justice. We give praise and ask help in living God's life as shining stars for others.

Lord God,
We are your people,
descendants as numerous as the stars in the sky.

Give us your *power* so we can continue the work of creation as we become your hands in building the earth. Our prayer response will be from Psalm 148:3;

> Praise God, sun and moon.
> Praise God, shining stars.

ALL: Praise God, sun and moon,
Praise God, shining stars.

LEADER: Give us your *wisdom*, so we may see your presence in the people we meet and in the work we do,
> Praise God, sun and moon,
> Praise God, shining stars.

ALL: Praise God, sun and moon,
Praise God, shining stars.

LEADER: Give us your *majesty*, so we may delight in the wonder of your earth and be filled with awe in the beauty of your people.
> Praise God, sun and moon.
> Praise God, shining stars.

ALL: Praise God, sun and moon,
Praise God, shining stars.

LEADER: Give us your *love*, so that our own hard hearts can be molded and shaped into loving concern and care for the poor and needy.
> Praise God, sun and moon.
> Praise God, shining stars.

ALL: Praise God, sun and moon,
Praise God, shining stars.

LEADER: Give us your *mercy*, so that in compassion we can reach out to heal the brokenhearted, forgive those we have hurt, and reconcile ourselves as your people.
> Praise God, sun and moon.
> Praise God, shining stars.

ALL: Praise God, sun and moon,
Praise God, shining stars.

LEADER: Give us your *justice*, so that the rights of all people around our planet earth are recognized and lived in freedom.
> Praise God, sun and moon.
> Praise God, shining stars.

ALL: Praise God, sun and moon,
Praise God, shining stars.

LEADER: Lord, we thank you for men and women in every nation who have become your light to others, for founders and leaders, presidents and governors, and all who work for peace, justice, and freedom. Give us shining constellations that show your presence in all people. We ask this in your name as creator, redeemer, and sustainer of all that you have made.

ALL: Amen.

Closing Blessing

(Pass filled toasting cups.)

LEADER: We each hold our cup in toast for America and her people, and for all countries and their people:
> My country, tis of thee,
> Sweet Land of Liberty, of thee I sing;
> Land where my fathers died.
> Land of the pilgrim's pride.
> From every mountain side
> Let freedom ring.

We toast for the ring of freedom everywhere and say, "Let freedom ring!"

ALL: Let freedom ring!

(All toast and drink.)

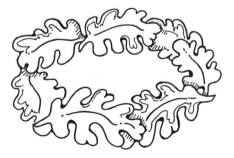

Earth Day

A Background Reflection

The arrival of spring, signaled by the vernal equinox about March 21, has always been a time for celebration. People once believed the earth mother as having the power to bring forth green plants to the earth each year, and engaged in rites to honor her. These rites were also performed to frighten away the demons of winter and help bring in summer. People were convinced that their rites played an essential part in having the sun warm the earth for seeds to grow.

Until the Gregorian calendar was introduced in 1582, spring also marked the beginning of the New Year. One can still see a similarity in the New Year and spring rites in many cultures today.

The use of water as a symbol of health and new life originated in the earliest festivals that honored the rebirth of the natural world. According to one ancient myth, the world began in water. In many parts of Europe, women washed their faces in the spring waters of brooks and rivers for this fresh water was considered to bring new life. In the Mideast, water is used as a sign of reconciliation: wheat, celery, or lentil seeds are placed in a bowl of water. Later, they are thrown into running water as a symbolic action of doing away with all family quarrels and starting the new year in friendliness and peace.

As the four seasons are symbolic of the rhythm of human life, the season of spring becomes rebirth, resurrection after the death of winter. Every tree and bush, every blade of grass, every flower is part of the miracle of life we celebrate each spring. For Christians, Easter is the celebration of Christ rising from the dead, a joyful celebration of resurrection and eternal life. Christ takes the place of the gods in ancient mythology who died and then returned to earth to bring new life to the world. Christ brings new life to the hearts of all.

Scripture begins with the creator God fashioning an earthly dwelling for us. And each step in creating is observed and judged to be good by the Creator. Genesis gives us two versions of creation; the second story speaks of a garden (symbol of divine blessings), a tree of life in the center of the garden (ancient symbol of immortality), and a flowing river that waters this garden earth and then flows to the four directions to nourish and sustain. Not only is the enjoyment of the garden a gift from God, but God even walks in the garden, giving a yet more intimate presence. In this second creation story, we are called to be caretakers of the garden that is earth.

Centuries have passed, and still today we not only ask God to bless us but we have become acutely aware that we have not lived up to our responsibility to be stewards of earth. As caretakers of the gifts of creation, we have become remiss. Environmental groups around the world have helped make us aware of the way in which we are misusing earth and depriving people of their basic rights to clear air, water, and food produced from our garden, Earth.

In April 1970, the first Earth Day was celebrated. It was a time to reawaken a spirit of thankfulness for the earth and its goods. The theme of the day was "Give Earth a Chance," and attention was given to our responsibility to reclaim the purity of air, water, and the living environment. A special tenth anniversary of this day was observed in 1980. Although no continuing organization exists for observance, the organizers hope there will be observances of Earth Day in different places at the time of the vernal equinox every year. For example, on March 20, 1979, children rang the United Nations peace bell in New York at the exact moment the sun crossed the equator.

Earth does not belong to any one people or any one nation, but is held in trust by every generation and is passed on as a legacy. Chief Seattle of the Suquamish Nation, in delivering his speech in 1854 when he was asked to turn his

Indian tribal lands over to the federal government said,

> Care for this land as we have cared for it, and with all your strength, with all your heart, preserve it for your children and love it as God loves all. No one owns the freshness of the air and the sparkle of the water. Every part of this earth is sacred to my people. Every shining pine needle, every sandy shore, every mist in the dark woods, every clearing, and every humming insect is holy in the memory and experience of my people.

Preparations

directions

Hang the green panel for the season of spring.

Place symbols of the garden Earth from the project below on this panel.

Choose seven readers.

Place a candle and a glass bowl of water before the panel. Use an evergreen bough for dipping and sprinkling the people.

Have names ready to give as you call each participant.

materials

Construction paper, butcher paper
Magic markers
Pins
Scissors

Project

Make an earth garden for a panel (large tree, plants, vegetables, grasses, vineyards, flowers, rivers flowing in four directions, etc.).Mark the seasons. Each participant designs and prints his or her name.

Cut it out and give it to the leader.

Prayer Celebration

Opening Greeting

LEADER: We gather to celebrate the gift of the earth in spring. Rivers flow.

ALL: So be it. So be it. So be it.

LEADER: Fruit trees flower.

ALL: So be it. So be it. So be it.

LEADER: Seeds sprout green.

ALL: So be it. So be it. So be it.

LEADER: Make us aware, Lord, of the grandeur of all creation and give us feet to walk humbly and hands to touch gently this garden earth. The gifts of God's garden earth be with you.

ALL: And also with you.

Garden Earth Readings and Promises

READER 1: "The Lord planted a garden in Eden, in the east, and there put the man God had formed. God made all kinds of beautiful trees. In the middle of the garden stood the tree that gives life. A stream flowed in Eden and watered the garden; and beyond Eden divided into four rivers. Then the Lord God placed the man in the garden to cultivate and guard it. Then the Lord God said, 'It is not good for you to live alone. I will make you a suitable companion to help you.' And the Lord God made woman."

Genesis 2:8–19 (adapted)

This is the Word of the Lord.

ALL: Thanks be to God.

LEADER: We know of God's presence as creator in our garden earth. Before our creation banner, we light this candle.

(pause)

May its flame warm the earth and each of our hearts. May this burning candle be a sign of God's presence with us always. As the earth is a gift, so we, created in the image and likeness of God, we, too, are a gift. We are gardeners of the earth, caretakers of the land. We cultivate and preserve; we guard and protect. As our name is called, we come forward to receive and place a sign of ourselves in our garden earth. _____(Name)_____, you are a gift. Care for this garden earth.

(Each person receives his or her name and places it on banner.)

READER 2: In our care for this garden earth, Lord, we will make our rivers, seas, and oceans, our brooks, streams, and lakes clean and fresh again. With your help, Lord, we will let them be a source of life for flowers, trees, and fish. For we will remember, that your gift of garden earth belongs to everyone.

ALL: So be it. So be it. So be it.

READER 3: In our care for this garden earth, Lord, we will plant fruit-bearing plants and vegetables, grasses, and bright-colored flowers. In tilled soil, we will cultivate vineyards and fields of grain. And the fullness of the harvest we will share with the poor who have little. For we will remember, that your gift of garden earth belongs to everyone.

ALL: So be it. So be it. So be it.

READER 4: In our care for this garden earth, Lord, we will preserve the freshness of clean air for all to breathe. We have a right to the smells of early morning and the scents of changing seasons. For we will remember that your gift of garden earth belongs to everyone.

ALL: So be it. So be it. So be it.

READER 5: In our care for this garden earth, Lord, we will respect our bodies by eating healthy foods, becoming physically fit, avoiding harmful products. Through prayer we will nourish our spirits and try to live simply as gardeners with each other. For we will remember that your gift of garden earth belongs to everyone.

ALL: So be it. So be it. So be it.

LEADER: Lord,
Thank you for the blessings of your garden earth. Inside each of us is a garden, also, a garden of your blessings. Inside each of us is the tree of life, a sign of life forever. Inside each of us the water of life, your life in us. Because of your presence may we come to know, care for, and love all the gardens of our life.

ALL: Amen.

Rite of Water

LEADER: Water is a sign of new life. A stream of life waters our garden and then flows into four rivers carrying God's life to the earth: north, south, east, and west. It is this same stream that gives drink to the city of God.

READER 6: "The river of the water of life, sparkling like crystal, flows down the middle of the city's street. On either side of the river is the tree of life, which bears fruit twelve times a year, once each month and its leaves are for the healing of the nations."

Revelations 22:1–2 (adapted)

This is the Word of the Lord.

ALL: Thanks be to God.

LEADER: We are like trees that grow beside a stream and bear fruit at the right time and whose leaves do not dry up.

READER 7: "A healthy tree does not bear bad fruit, nor does a poor tree bear good fruit. Every tree is known by the fruit it bears; you do not pick figs from thorn bushes or gather grapes from bramble bushes. A good person brings good out of the treasure of good things in her heart."

Luke 6:43–45 GNB (adapted)

LEADER: We come to our water to bless ourselves for the good fruit we will bear to others through all the months of the year.

(Water bowl is carried to each person, who dips a finger into the water and makes a self blessing in the sign of the cross; appropriate music could be played.)

Closing Blessing: Blessing of Garden Earth

LEADER: Christ is the light of our spring, the life of our garden earth, the living water that nourishes. Soon we will celebrate the paschal mystery of living, dying, and rising. At Easter, gardeners of the earth will join voices and hearts as we proclaim,
"Jesus is our Risen Lord! Alleluia!"
We bless this garden earth to receive the risen Lord. We bless all rivers.

(Dip and sprinkle water.)

ALL: Amen.

LEADER: We bless all trees.

(Dip and sprinkle water.)

LEADER: We bless all seeds.

(Dip and sprinkle water.)

ALL: Amen.

LEADER: We bless north, south, east, and west.

(Dip and sprinkle water.)

ALL: Amen.

LEADER: We bless the hearts of our faithful gardeners.

(Dip and sprinkle water.)

ALL: Amen.

LEADER: In joy and gladness, we say yes to the season of spring as we celebrate this festival of our garden earth.

ALL: So be it. So be it. So be it.

Palm Sunday

A Background Reflection

Palm Sunday commemorates the triumphal entry of Jesus into Jerusalem. The gospel records that people welcomed Jesus as king as they spread their cloaks before him, waved olive branches, and loudly praised the Lord with these words:

> Hosanna to the Son of David!
> Blessed is he who comes in the name of the Lord!
> Hosanna in the highest!

Matthew 21:9 RSV

The earliest record of the ritual of Palm Sunday comes from the fourth-century travel journal of the nun Etheria. In Jerusalem, on the eve of the Lord's day, she observed that as people walked the streets, children were carried on their parents' shoulders, and the old and young alike waved palm or olive branches as they sang.

This custom of Palm Sunday soon spread throughout the Western church. As the ritual developed, a blessing and the distribution of palm branches were added to the procession. We see the same ritual today in many of our churches, with the reading of the Passion following the procession. The custom of burning leftover palm leaves and using these ashes on Ash Wednesday the following year still persists in many churches.

Since palm trees do not grow in every country, places like England once referred to this Sunday as Olive Sunday, Branch Sunday, Sunday of the Willow Boughs, while Germany used the name Blossom Sunday. And even though palms grow in Mexico, for example, the people walked carrying flowers and laurels. After receiving a blessing, families placed these branches in their homes until the following year, as protection against illness.

Even today, many southern cities in the United States have adapted the French custom of placing blessed palms on graves of their loved ones. And palms placed in the home today, sometimes behind a crucifix or holy picture or simply fastened to a wall, remind us of the palms placed in homes centuries ago, which were thought to offer protection against storms and lightning or bestow a home blessing for the people.

Like the blessing and distribution of palms, processions were integral to the early Palm Sunday ritual. One procession had a priest riding a donkey in imitation of Jesus while people placed leaves and branches along the path. The procession moved into Church with the opening of the gates or doors, reminiscent of Psalm 23:9: "Open wide the doors and gates—the King of Glory enters." In some European villages, these processions ended in the performance of a mystery play that continued to recreate the events of Holy Week.

Today processions are usually performed in church after the blessing of palms. The people then walk around the church waving palms and singing. Some churches observe the ancient service of Tenebrae, in which candles are extinguished during sung antiphons. There has been an increased interest in churches joining for ecumenical rites on this Sunday.

The theme of peace for Palm Sunday was once reflected in the Pax (peace) cakes of England. People who had quarreled during the year were invited to come and eat those cakes as they tried to understand each other's problems. Like the palm branches in Italy offered to another as a token of forgiveness and peace, we are reminded of our call to change our hearts and reconcile our differences as we enter Holy Week.

Preparations

directions

Hang the green panel for the season of spring. Place the word *Hosanna* on it. Decorate with colored streamers.

Put four lighted candles at the foot of this panel. (You may want to use your Yule Wheel if you have one.)

Choose two narrators.

Designate four stations (spaces or corners of a room) as areas for the journey. The fourth station is before the green panel. Place signs to indicate these four areas.

Place the donkey near Station One.

Have palms, pussy willows, boxwood, whatever is available in your area for the blessing of the branches and procession. After they are blessed, ask someone to place them at Station Three.

Choose someone to extinguish one candle after each station.

For the play, designate participants to be Jesus, two disciples, and someone to carry the "donkey." The other participants are the crowd. Everyone proceeds through the four stations.

materials

Four candles, (Yule Wheel, optional)
Green panel
Construction paper, crepe paper
Cardboard or poster board
Magic markers

Project

Make a donkey and place on a stick. Make signs to denote the different stations. Place the word *Hosanna* on the banner and hang colored streamers from the bottom or side.

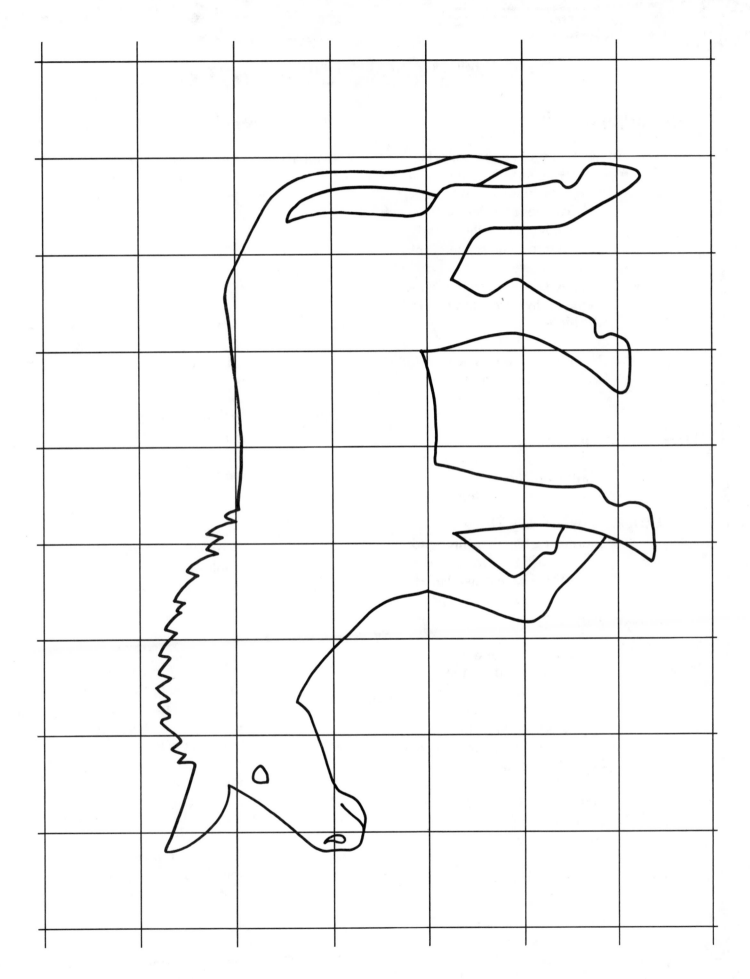

33

Prayer Celebration

Opening Greeting

LEADER: Jesus has told us how special we are. Now is the time to tell everyone how special Jesus is. Our candles of welcome have been lighted. Like the crowd received Jesus on his entry into Jerusalem, we say, "Hosanna! Blessed is he who comes in the name of the Lord. Hosanna in the highest!"

ALL: Hosanna! Blessed is he who comes in the name of the Lord. Hosanna in the highest!

Blessing of Branches

(Gather branches—pussy willows, boxwood, palms—and so on.)

LEADER: Dear friends, we have been journeying together throughout the days of Lent. On this road of faith, we have walked in a spirit of prayer and loving service to others.
Let us pray:
Lord, God, creator of the universe and maker of all things, we ask you to bless these branches. Make these branches holy. May the carrying of these branches give honor to Jesus as he enters the city of Jerusalem to complete his work as Messiah—to suffer, to die, and to rise again. Jesus is Lord forever and ever!

ALL: Jesus is Lord forever and ever!

(In silence the branches are sprinkled with water and placed at Station One.)

The Gospel Drama Reading

NARRATOR 1: Come. Take your places. We are going to walk the road to Jerusalem and enter the city with Jesus.

(Participants as crowd move to Station One.)

Toward Station One

NARRATOR 1: As the crowd drew near to Jerusalem, Jesus called two of his disciples and asked them to do him a favor.

NARRATOR 2: "Go into the village straight ahead of you. There you will find a donkey. Untie the donkey and bring it to me. Now if anyone says a word to you, I want you to say, 'The master needs it!' Then the people will let you have the donkey at once. Now go and do as I have asked."

(Two disciples leave. Jesus joins crowd.)

NARRATOR 1: A long time ago it had been said by one of the prophets that your King comes to you with pomp and pageantry, without royal purple robes. He comes to you meek and lowly, riding upon a donkey.

NARRATOR 2: The two disciples return with the donkey. Jesus comes and sits on the donkey. As our road journey with Jesus begins, our first candle goes out.

(pause)

Toward Station Two

NARRATOR 1: The journey continues. Some of the crowd spread their cloaks on the road. It was said that "the children of Jerusalem welcomed Christ the King. They spread their cloaks before him and loudly praised the Lord. "Hosanna to the Son of David!"

ALL: Hosanna to the Son of David!

NARRATOR 1: Blessed is he who comes in the name of the Lord.

ALL: Blessed is he who comes in the name of the Lord.

NARRATOR 1: Hosanna in the highest!

ALL: Hosanna in the highest!

NARRATOR 1: Before the road journey continues, our second candle goes out.

(pause)

Toward Station Three

NARRATOR 2: As the crowd continues walking along the road, they shout, "Hosanna, Hosanna, Hosanna!"

ALL: Hosanna, Hosanna, Hosanna!

NARRATOR 2: Hosanna in the highest!

ALL: Hosanna in the highest!

NARRATOR 1: The crowd stops, and some of the people cut branches from the trees. They hold these branches in their hands and then begin waving them in the air.

(The blessed branches are used here.)

The people were happy. They wanted to tell Jesus how special he was. And so they shouted, "Hosanna to the Son of David!"

ALL: Hosanna to the Son of David!

NARRATOR 1: It was said that the children of Jerusalem welcomed Christ the King. They carried olive branches and loudly praised the Lord: "Hosanna in the highest!"

ALL: Hosanna in the highest!

NARRATOR 1: And before the road journey continues, our third candle goes out.

(pause)

Toward Station Four

NARRATOR 2: And the crowd continued walking on the road. As Jesus enters the city of Jerusalem, the whole city was amazed and asked, "Who is this?" and the crowd that was following Jesus kept answering, "This is the prophet Jesus from Nazareth in Galilee."

ALL: This is the prophet Jesus from Nazareth in Galilee.

NARRATOR 1: And together the crowd rejoiced. They waved their branches and praised God with one loud voice, "Blessed is he who comes as king in the name of the Lord!"

ALL: Blessed is he who comes as king in the name of the Lord!

NARRATOR 2: Peace in heaven and glory in the highest!

ALL: Peace in heaven and glory in the highest!

NARRATOR 1: And the fourth candle is extinguished.

(pause)

Jerusalem Prayer of Peace

(standing before panel)

LEADER: Our response will be "We come in the name of the Lord and we walk in peace."

ALL: We come in the name of the Lord and we walk in peace.

LEADER: Lord, You have come to give us Your peace. In that peace, we go to the brokenhearted and lonely, and we say,

ALL: We come in the name of the Lord and we walk in peace.

LEADER: We go to the poor and powerless, and we say,

ALL: We come in the name of the Lord and we walk in peace.

LEADER: We go to the neglected and ignored, and we say,

ALL: We come in the name of the Lord and we walk in peace.

LEADER: We go to those who have hurt us with unkind words and actions, and we say,

ALL: We come in the name of the Lord and we walk in peace.

LEADER: We go to those we have hurt, asking forgiveness, and we say,

ALL: We come in the name of the Lord and we walk in peace.

LEADER: Long ago it was the custom to wave palms over one another as a blessing of peace. We each hold our palms over the head of the person in front of us and bless that person as a peacemaker in our world.

(Pause and everyone holds a branch over someone else's head.)

Bless you.

ALL: **Bless you.**

LEADER: **You are holy.**

ALL: **You are holy.**

LEADER: **Bless you.**

ALL: **Bless you.**

LEADER: **You are a peacemaker.**

ALL: **You are a peacemaker.**

LEADER: **We bless Jesus, wave our palms as we say,**

ALL: **Holy, holy, holy, Lord God of power and might, heaven and earth are full of your glory. Hosanna in the highest! Blessed is he who comes in the name of the Lord. Hosanna in the highest!**

LEADER: **As we walked the road to Jerusalem with loud shouts of joy, so now we become quiet.**

(Pause until all are quiet.)

We are beginning Holy Week. Our once-lit candles are in darkness. As a sign of our need for reconciliation and peace in our life, we exchange branches with one another.

(Everyone exchanges branches.)

We silently go forth to bring our branches to the homebound, the sick, the elderly, and to our own homes. May this branch in our home be a sign of the peace Jesus gives us through his living, dying, and rising.

ALL: **Amen.**

(Everyone quietly leaves.)

Matthew 21:1–11 (adapted)

37

April Fool's Day

A Background Reflection

On the first of April the world is turned upside down and order is made topsy-turvy. Things are not what they seem. April Fool's Day becomes a splendid celebration of the ridiculous.

On April Fool's Day we play tricks on people. The actual origins of the day have never been determined. However, the timing of April Fool's Day is appropriate because at this time of the year we are often fooled by capricious weather changes. Some people think this day is a relic of an ancient Roman feast in honor of Ceres, whose daughter, Prosperpina, was carried off by Pluto and made his queen. Ceres' search for her daughter was considered a "fool's errand." Or perhaps the custom began in India: in the spring festival Huli people are sent on foolish errands and they throw colored powder and water on one another. Sweets are exchanged, and groups gather in the street to sing and dance.

According to one version, the April date of this fool's holiday is derived from France, following the Gregorian calendar change of 1582, when the New Year was moved from March 25 to January 1. Gifts had always been exchanged during the New Year season, which ended on April 1. Many people did not like the new date, while others simply forgot the change and they were called fools as they continued gift giving on April 1. Others kept the custom of sending gifts on that day but the gifts were silly, worthless, and packaged to look like something they were not.

In France, young fish appear in the rivers early in April, fish that are easier to catch than the older ones. A silly or easily tricked person was called *poisson d'avril*, which means "April fish," since that person "bites" on the joke bait and is "caught." April fools are still called that in France, and the custom of giving children a chocolate fish continues. French children play jokes on one another as we do in the United States. By the way, a fish is also a symbol for Christ, because the ancient Greek word for fish,

ichthys, is an acronym for Christ's name [i] Jesus, [ch] Christ, [th] God's [y] Son, [s] Savior.

Soon the tricks and fool's errands spread from France to England. People were told to wait for the hour when a statue would descend from its pedestal, to buy a left-handed hammer, to get a pint of pigeon's milk, some sweet vinegar, or a stick with one end.

During medieval European festivals, the noble lord or lady presiding became jester and was called Lord or Lady of Misrule. Dressed in a foolish costume of many colors, the presider wore a long, floppy, double-pointed hat with bells at its tips. Everything from serving food to reading, to game playing, to dancing, was done backwards.

Many people think that April Fool's Day was once joined to a church holiday called the Feast of Fools. A young boy would dress in bishop's clothes, give a sermon, and lead a discussion of religious doctrine, handing out praise or punishment according to the response of participants. Similarly, today, students are sometimes invited to take over the instruction of the class.

The Feast of the Donkey in France possibly derived from the Feast of Fools. Short plays depicting the adventures of the prophet Balaam and his wondrous donkey are presented. In this story the world is turned around as the donkey becomes the protector and speaks to the foolish prophet in a wise manner. Sometimes, different plays of other famous donkeys from Scriptures were told, with particular emphasis given to the donkey that stood at the manger and carried Jesus and Mary to Egypt.

In one short movie, *The Parable*, the main character representing Christ is a clown. And St. Paul describes himself as a fool for Christ. (1 Corinthians 4:10), while Francis of Assisi and Ignatius of Loyola speak of the "foolishness" of the Gospel, which they and their followers tried to live in their own lifestyle. Jesus' own relatives said he had gone mad (Mark 3:31), and he was treated as a fool by Herod (Luke 22:8–12), by his mockers during his passion (Mark 15:16–20), and even on Calvary (Luke 23:35–38). It is interesting that the Eastern Church has one category of saint not present in our Western Church: the fool.

In a sense, should we not be convinced with the apostle Paul that it is through the foolishness of the cross that God's wisdom triumphs over human wisdom (1 Corinthians 1:11–2:29)? Is not the resurrection God's surprise for all creation? Are we not in our daily lives startled, surprised by the Spirit?

It is no accident that we find clown and fool ministry among Christian groups committed to peace and justice. It was once the role of the court fool to represent alternatives to the royal policies. In nonviolent resistance to what is dehumanizing in our world, do we not as Christians learn to "play the fool."

European settlers brought April Fool's customs to the American colonies. Today people still call the zoo asking for Mr. Fox, tell younger brothers and sisters they have (nonexistent) stains on their shirts, and send unsuspecting people to the library for a biography of Eve's mother.

Perhaps there is sense to all this nonsense. It is true that rules are sometimes uncomfortable for us to follow, but after a day of disorder, with our world turned upside down, life would be even worse. After the amusement of April Fool's Day, people more willingly turn their attention to living a life right side up.

Preparations

directions

Hang the green panel for the season of spring. Place a basket of fish before it (the fish can be made of construction paper—you may also wish to add some chocolate candies).

Have a jester's hat ready for presentation and place before the green panel during the Opening Greeting.

Assign parts to participants: Balaam, the donkey, King Balak, his people, two messengers, two princes, an angel.

Familiarize different characters with gestures and movement they will be doing. As the leader, be prepared to pause for actions marked in parentheses.

Choose and place signs for three locations: Area 1 (Balaam's place), Area 2 (King's place), Area 3 (A Road).

materials

Chocolate pieces or paper fish for each participant
Material for costumes
Construction paper
Scissors, magic markers, staplers or tape
Sticks

Project

Make a jester's hat.

Make construction paper signs for characters like those below. Staple or tape each sign to a stick. (Or choose costumes for the different characters to wear.)

Make a sword for the angel.

Make signs for three areas: Balaam's place, King's place, a road.

Make construction paper fish. Have each participant put his or her name on a fish and the words "Caught by God's Love."

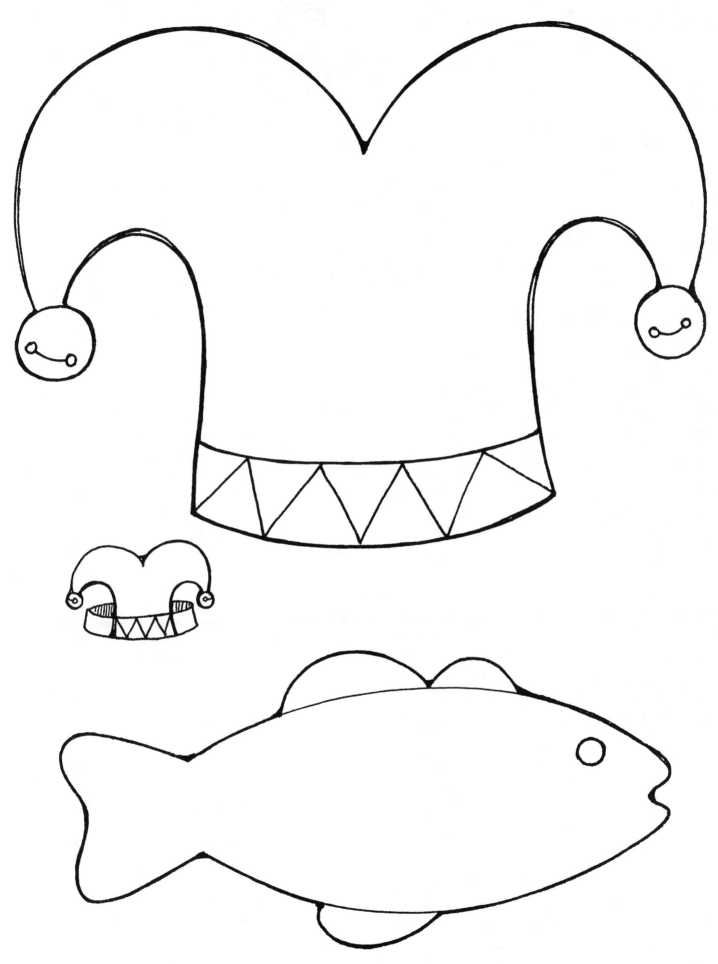

Prayer Celebration

Opening Greeting

LEADER: Welcome to a celebration of the foolish, the one day of the year when life is seen turned around and upside down, when things are not as they should be. Welcome to the Feast of Fools.

(Present jester's hat.)

The Donkey Story

LEADER: Let us listen to a story where the expected becomes the unexpected, and a donkey speaks and becomes the protector of his owner. It is a story from the book of Numbers that was told long ago on this day.

In Area 1

LEADER: Once there was a prophet Balaam.

(Balaam walks out.)

Balaam had an animal friend, a donkey, who was good, gentle and kind.

(Donkey walks out.)

Everyday Balaam groomed his animal friend.

(Balaam grooms donkey.)

Sometimes Balaam, as a prophet, would lift his hand and pronounce a blessing on the people.

(Balaam raises hand in blessing.)

And when he did this, you knew people were blessed. Sometimes he would stretch out his hand and pronounce a curse.

(Balaam turns hand over.)

And when he did this, you knew people were cursed.

In Area 2

LEADER: Now it came to pass that one day the Israelites set up camp in the land of King Balak.

(Set up camp.)

The king and all his people were terrified.

(fear and trembling)

"There are too many Israelites. Surely they will eat all that grows on our land." So the king sent messengers to Balaam with these words: "Come curse these people, so the king can drive them out of our land."

(Messengers travel to Area 1.)

In Area 1

LEADER: Balaam welcomed the messengers with kindness.

(action)

But his animal friend did not. He brayed, he jumped about.

(action)

Balaam said, "Spend the night here. In the morning I will report to you what the Lord tells me. The messengers went to sleep.

(snoring heard)

Balaam prayed.

(action)

And God said to Balaam (whisper), "Do not go with these men. Do not put a curse on the people of Israel. They have my blessing." The next morning, Balaam sent the messenger home.

(Messengers travel to Area 2 as Balaam points way.)

And Balaam's animal friend was happy.

(donkey jumping)

In Area 2

LEADER: They told the king, "Balaam refuses to come here." The king would not accept this. This time the king sent princes with gifts.

(Travel to Area 1.)

In Area 1

LEADER: On arrival, the princes pleaded, "Please come and curse these people so the king can drive them out of our land."

(on knees pleading)

Balaam welcomed these messengers with kindness.

(action)

But his animal friend did not. He brayed and jumped about.

(action)

Again Balaam said, "Spend the night here. In the morning I will report to you what the Lord tells me." The messengers went to sleep.

(snoring heard)

Balaam prayed. And God said to him (whisper), "Go with them, but do only what I tell you." The next morning Balaam saddled his donkey and went with the princes.

In Area 3

LEADER: As Balaam was riding his animal friend, an angel of the Lord suddenly appeared.

(action)

The donkey saw the angel holding a sword and quickly tried to run into the fields.

(donkey running)

Because Balaam did not see the angel, he beat the donkey back onto the road.

(action)

They continued traveling.

(walking in place)

Suddenly the angel stood where the road was narrow with a stone wall on each side.

(Angel appears.)

The donkey saw the angel and moved against the wall, hurting Balaam's leg. Balaam screamed out.

(Ahhhhh . . .)

Because Balaam did not see the angel, he beat the donkey again.

(beating)

They continued traveling.

(walking in place)

Suddenly, the angel appeared again. This time the donkey lay down. Balaam lost his temper. He began to beat the donkey with a stick. The donkey brayed. And Balaam beat him harder. And suddenly speech came to the donkey and he said, "What have I done to you? Why have you beaten me three times with a stick?" And Balaam answered, "Because you have made a fool of me." "Am I not the same donkey who has been faithful to you all your life?" Suddenly, God opened Balaam's eyes to see the angel. Balaam fell to the ground and asked forgiveness. God told him to continue his journey but to refuse to curse the people when he arrived. "Tell the king that I love the Israelites," was God's message to Balaam. "Give them my blessing." Balaam went home — happy in God's blessing. His donkey went home — happy also with God's blessing.

Numbers 22 (adapted)

The Sending

LEADER: Sometimes we allow ourselves to be sent on foolish errands by others. When God sends us, as Balaam was sent, it is never foolish. We are sent by God to bring blessing and healing to a troubled world. And God asks, "Who will go to the lonely and frightened, the unloved and unwanted?" And we say, "Here I am Lord, send me."

ALL: Here I am, Lord, send me.

LEADER: "Who will go to the troubled and depressed, the sad and grieving?" And we say, "Here I am Lord, send me."

ALL: Here I am, Lord, send me.

LEADER: Who will go to the lost and wandering, the confused and misunderstood? And we say, "Here I am, Lord, send me."

ALL: Here I am, Lord, send me.

LEADER: "Who will go to the poor and frail, the sick and dying?" And we say, "Here I am, Lord, send me."

ALL: Here I am, Lord, send me.

LEADER: "Who will feed my people, give them drink and shelter, welcome them into their hearts and homes?" And we say, "Here I am, Lord, send me."

ALL: Here I am, Lord, send me.

LEADER: "Who will go and tell the people that I love them forever?" And we say, "Here I am, Lord, send me."

ALL: Here I am, Lord, send me.

LEADER: Lord, bless us in all your sendings. As your messengers, we run with glad hearts to speak of your presence in our life and to offer your blessing through us to others. May you always send us on errands of your love.

ALL: Amen.

A Reading

LEADER: In scripture, Paul speaks of the way we can tolerate fools in our life, and how we can accept ourselves as fools for Christ.

READER: "I beg you to follow our example.
For Christ's sake we are fools.
We are weak, but you are strong.
We are despised but you are honored.
We go hungry and thirsty;
we are clothed in rags. We wander from place to place.
We wear ourselves out with hard work.
We bless when we are cursed.
We endure when we are persecuted.
We answer back with kind words when we are insulted.
I beg you to follow our example.
For Christ's sake, become a fool."

1 Corinthians 4:10–13 GNB (adapted)

This is the Word of the Lord.

ALL: Thanks be to God.

Closing Blessing

LEADER: Long ago it was the custom to give children a chocolate fish on April Fool's Day. Just as small fish in the early spring were easily caught, so fish represents all of us readily caught by God's love. We pass our basket of fish.

(pause)

Let us bow our head for God's blessing. May the beauty of God's creation always startle us.

ALL: Amen.

LEADER: May the goodness of Jesus's life always challenge us.

ALL: Amen.

LEADER: May the love of the Spirit's power always surprise us.

ALL: Amen.

LEADER: Thank you, Lord God, for showing us how to be a fool like Christ in love of your people. We go forth now on your errand of love.

ALL: Amen.

Good Friday

A Background Reflection

The anniversary of the passion and death of Christ is commemorated on Friday of Holy Week —Good Friday. Since the life of Christ, Good Friday has been celebrated as a day of sadness, mourning, fasting, and prayer. For Catholics, Good Friday and Ash Wednesday are the only two remaining days when the church asks members to fast.

There are many different rituals for Good Friday. A three-hour devotion is popular in both Catholic and Protestant churches and consists of meditations on the seven last words Jesus spoke from the cross. Hymns are usually sung between these meditations.

The Adoration of the Cross is another Good Friday devotion. During the Adoration of the Cross, people kneel, bow, and prostrate themselves three times as they advance toward the cross. In Catholic churches today, the presider unveils the crucifix in three stages while singing, "This is the wood of the cross on which hung the Savior of the world." The people are then invited to come forth and kiss the feet of the image.

Besides the Adoration of the Cross, the Stations of the Cross are offered on Good Friday by many churches. It is said that during the Crusades Christians visiting Jerusalem marked off the sites where they thought the Christ's passion had occurred. On returning home, these travelers continued this devotion by erecting memorials of these stations inside their churches or outside in their fields. Today, many Catholic and Episcopal churches have carvings of these passion scenes on their walls.

St. Augustine said that from the moment of Christ's death to the morning of his resurrection was forty hours. From this forty-hour "wake" grew the Forty Hours devotion of fast and prayer that became popular at other chosen times of the year. This devotion is still honored in many churches today.

To commemorate Good Friday, many home observances among families have been faithfully followed. In England plain rice cooked in milk became the traditional Good Friday meal, while the Irish had their "black fast" of only water or tea for the day. In central Europe, vegetable soup and bread were eaten standing and in silence. Today, many people fast, eating only rice during the day or soup at night. A mood of silence continues to permeate the day. Church altars are stripped bare; so are many kitchen tables, left with only a cactus plant as a centerpiece.

The custom of making and eating hot cross buns on Good Friday dates back to pagan days, when tiny cakes were offered to the goddess known as the Queen of Heaven. Made of spiced dough, round in shape, with a cross of icing on top, hot cross buns to commemorate Easter became popular in Europe and later in America. The buns were considered blessed. If eaten on Good Friday, they protected you against sickness and dangers such as house fires and lightning. Some people would keep a hot cross bun throughout the year in their home and eat it as medicine or wear as a charm. From the hot cross bun developed the widespread custom of marking a new loaf of bread with the sign of the cross before cutting it.

Actually, many popular observances once done in a spirit of true reverence later gave rise to superstitions. For example, it was said that craftspeople were not to swing hammers or drive nails on the day Christ was nailed to a cross, and people were not to use instruments made of iron. So carpenters, plumbers, and blacksmiths did not work on Good Friday. Vinegar, used to mock Jesus' thirst on the cross, was eliminated from the day's menus. Washing clothes on Good Friday, was supposed to bring bad luck for the year. In Spain developed the custom of dipping up water from wells or rivers before sunrise without speaking. This gesture was thought to have healing power and to ensure that the people's source of water would remain pure all year. From Central Europe came the ritual of planting parsley, beans, and peas for a good year's crop. Superstitions are not "true," but they do reflect people's need for tradition, symbolism, and ritual.

Today people also need some tangible things to do—or not to do—in giving focus to this day. For example, early Christians refused to greet anyone on Good Friday with *Shalom* ("peace be with you"), for this was what Judas said in betraying Jesus. They would only use the greeting "the Light of God be with you." So we look to find rituals to mark this day.

We mark the anniversary of the death of someone close to us through rituals—lighting a candle, celebrating the Eucharist, visiting the grave. And we share stories about that person— we remember again that person's presence in our lives. On Good Friday, too, we can remember how Jesus has touched our lives in the past and speak, through stories, of Jesus' continued presence in our lives.

Preparations

directions

Hang the green panel for the spring season. Make and display a cross of bare branches.

Choose readers for a boy with loaves and fishes, a woman in a crowd, the daughter of Jairus, Peter, Mary Magdalene, and Mary. Each has a sign to place before the cross.

Acquaint participants on how to bow, bending from waist, with reverence before the cross.

Have slips of paper and pencils, pens, or markers ready for Your Remembrance section. On their completion during ceremony, collect these slips in basket.

Place hot cross buns before the cross.

Choose appropriate instrumental music.

You may want to hold the branch cross for the closing blessing.

materials

Green panel
Bare branches
Twine
Paper
Pens, pencils, magic markers

Project

With twine, make a cross from bare, found branches. Make loaves and fishes, the word *help*, a hand, fishing net, stones, a heart, for each of the readers.

Make or buy hot cross buns.

Prayer Celebration

Opening Greeting

LEADER: This is a memorial to our Lord;
this is the anniversary of the
passion and death of Christ.
As we stand before this simple
cross, we remember what
Jesus did for us—
he died for us,
he rose,
and he will come again.
We bow before your cross
Lord, and say,
"We adore you, O Lord,"

ALL: We adore you, O Lord.

LEADER: "And we bless you"

ALL: And we bless you

LEADER: "Because by your holy cross"

ALL: Because by your holy cross

LEADER: "You have redeemed the
world."

ALL: You have redeemed the world.

Francis of Assisi

In Remembrance

LEADER: We speak from our hearts of
the way Jesus has touched our
life. These words are spoken in
remembrance of Jesus by
people who knew him. Their
words become our tribute to
Jesus.

LITTLE BOY WITH LOAVES AND FISHES: "People sometimes say that
when you are little you cannot
do much. But this is not
always true. It does not matter
how old you are when you are
able to share. One day I was
hungry. My Mom had given
me lunch but I saved it while I
listened to Jesus talk. It started
getting late. I heard someone
asking if anyone had any food.
The people were hungry. Of
course I gave my bread and
fish. Wouldn't you? Jesus was
giving to the people by
comforting them and helping
them to love themselves
again. Even if it was not much,
I wanted to give something,
too. That is how I remember
Jesus—outside in an open
field—giving to the people."

LEADER: We thank the little boy with
the loaves and fishes for his
words of remembrance.
Before the cross, he bows and
places a sign of giving in his
life and in the life of Jesus.

(pause as boy does so)

And someone else remembers
Jesus.

A WOMAN IN THE CROWD: "I saw people trying to touch
him. He even had to go out in
a boat, for the crowds were so
great. I don't know why I was
there, just a face in the crowd,
but these people were there
because they believed in him.
Many were cured—deaf to
hear, blind to see, lame to
walk, those in sadness were
joyful again, those in doubt

now believed. I did not know why I had followed the crowd, why I was there. But suddenly I knew that I wanted to be free, I wanted to ask for help. And I did. And I was helped. That's how I remember Jesus — helping others and helping me."

LEADER: We thank a face in the crowd for her words of remembrance. Before the cross she bows and places a sign of helping in her life and in the life of Jesus.

(pause as woman does so)

And someone else remembers Jesus.

DAUGHTER OF JAIRUS: "Once I was so sick my father went looking for Jesus to see if he could help me. My father was an important man in our village. But when he found Jesus he fell on his knees and begged him to come to me. My father loved me very much; so did Jesus, for he came right away. They tell me he stretched out his hand over me, and said some words of blessing. I remember opening my eyes and looking at his face — it was so kind and compassionate. He told the people to feed me and to take care of me. That is how I remember Jesus — caring for me and asking others to show that same care.

LEADER: We thank the little daughter of Jairus for her words of remembrance. Before the cross, she bows and places a

sign of caring in her life and in the life of Jesus.

(pause as daughter does so)

And someone else remembers Jesus.

PETER: "What can I say? I began to sink in the water because I did not believe. After hesitating with Jesus's request to throw the net over again after we have been fishing all night and had caught nothing, I fell on my knees when the net was full. I said I would never deny Jesus and I did — three times. And through all my doubts, he never stopped loving me and never stopped asking me to love others. He believed in me more than I believed in myself. That is how I remember Jesus — believing in me and accepting me in my strengths and weaknesses."

LEADER: We thank Peter for his words of remembrance. Before the cross, he bows and places a sign of believing in his life and in the life of Jesus.

(pause as Peter does so)

And someone else remembers Jesus.

MARY MAGDALENE: "I have known joy in my life, and sadness, too. Even when I had done many wrong things and people wanted to stone me, Jesus rescued me. He forgave me, too. I was never the same again. I became his faithful friend — helped him as best I could as he did the work of God. I knew he had to die. But I just could not believe it. The memory of that Friday is still deep within me. I do not know how I was ever able to stand there at the foot of the cross. I cried. That is how I remember Jesus—loving and forgiving others, even his enemies, before he died."

LEADER: We thank Mary Magdalene for her words of remembrance. Before the cross she bows and places a sign of forgiveness in her life and in the life of Jesus.

(pause as the Magdalene does so)

And someone else remembers Jesus.

MARY: "I held him as a baby in my arms—helped him to learn how to walk. And all during those thirty years, before he even began his ministry, I wondered what would happen to this son of mine. His compassion for people was so beautiful. I was there at Cana when he changed water to wine. I was there when he healed and comforted the people. I was there in Jerusalem for the Passover. And I was there when he died on the cross. And when they took him down from the cross, I held him in my arms, just like I once did when he was a baby. My son. What love you have for others. That is how I remember Jesus—as a mother remembers her son."

LEADER: We thank Mary for her words of remembrance. Before the cross she bows and places a sign of love in her life and in the life of Jesus.

(pause as Mary does so)

Your Remembrance

LEADER: What is your remembrance of Jesus?

(pause)

How would you speak of Jesus?

(pause)

How do you need Jesus in your life right now?

(pause)

On your paper, draw or write a sign or words for the way you remember Jesus.

(Music plays as these signs are made and collected by passed baskets.)

The Cross

LEADER: "Jesus was led away, and carrying his cross by himself set out to what is called Golgotha." (John 19:17). The cross is a sign of Jesus's love for us, a sign of his willingness to forgive us forever. Let Jesus carry your needs, carry your wrongdoings, carry your faults and weaknesses. That is why Jesus carried his cross—for you. That is why Jesus died—for you. Think of one wrongdoing, one weakness in which you are in need of forgiveness.

(pause)

In procession, let each of us go forth, bow before the cross, and as we touch the cross mentally place our wrongdoing on the cross.

(pause)

Jesus carried our sins, but he does not carry the memory of them. Forgiven, we are free to live for others and so we bow and say, "We adore you, O Lord, and we bless you,"

ALL: We adore you, O Lord, and we bless you,

LEADER: "Because by your cross you have redeemed the world.

ALL: Because by your cross you have redeemed the world.

A Psalm

LEADER: In gratitude and thanksgiving, and in the memory of Jesus, we pray his prayer to his father. Our response will be, "Father, I put my life in your hands."

ALL: Father, I put my life in your hands.

LEADER: In you, O Lord, I find protection
Rescue me when I am afraid.
Redeem me when I am ashamed.
In your hands, O Lord, I place my spirit.

ALL: Father, I put my life in your hands.

LEADER: Sometimes people make fun of me.
They laugh and turn their backs on me.
Sometimes I feel like a dish that is broken
for I am forgotten and not important to anyone.

ALL: Father, I put my life in your hands.

LEADER: I trust you, my Lord.
In faith I say, "You are my God."
Rescue me from people who want to hurt me.
In your hands hold me and love me.

ALL: Father, I put my life in your hands.

LEADER: Let your face shine bright upon me.
May your kindness and gentleness save me.
Give me courage and make me fearless.
In your hands, O Lord, I place my hope.

ALL: Father, I put my life in your hands."

Psalm 31 (adapted)

Closing Blessing

LEADER: As for the people of long ago, our hot cross buns remind us that we are bound to one another through the cross of Jesus. We break and pass one of our hot cross buns.

(pause

As we eat this bread, we pledge our willingness to help carry the burdens of others as Jesus carries us. Bow your head for God's blessing. Through the cross you brought joy to the world.

ALL: Amen.

LEADER: Through the cross we remember the way you gave your life to us.

ALL: Amen.

LEADER: Through the cross you carry our burdens.

ALL: Amen.

LEADER: In the name of God the creator,
the Son the redeemer,
and the Holy Spirit the life giver,
we go forth to carry the burdens of others.

ALL: Amen.

(Share and eat the hot cross buns.)

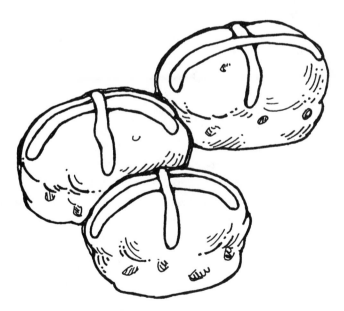

May Day

A Background Reflection

We are one earth and this oneness extends to all that makes this earth—people, flowers, trees, rhythm of the seasons, water, fire, air. We befriend all the elements of life, for together we travel this life journey. It is in the spirit of this befriending that the ancients tried in the rituals of May Day to reawaken spring and alert the spirits of fields and forests to a new season.

One ritual, the May Pole or May Tree, probably has its origin in prehistoric times. Trees have always been symbols of great vitality and fertility so it was natural to use them at spring festivals. The May tree was crowned with garlands of leaves and flowers, brightly colored ribbons wound around its shaft, and bells—to awaken the sleeping earth—placed on its branches.

Around the Maypole, the May Queen led the people in circle dances. Periodically the movement would stop and everyone would lift his or her right foot in the air and then stamp it down again, to reawaken the earth. A different girl was chosen and crowned with flowers each year. The choice was based on how well she represented a particular quality. From this custom derived the May Crownings of Mary (mother of Christ) and the song "Queen of the May" that accompanied this ritual.

In medieval May Day festivals, the circular evergreen May wreath, like the modern Christmas or Advent wreath, was often placed on doors and in windows. Sometimes large hoops were decorated with green ribbons and bells, then suspended from ceilings. For a costume, a crown of green leaves with flowers were worn and a green ribbon (a baldric) was placed over the right shoulder, crossing the chest and back diagonally and tying at the left hip. Even the food served at these festivals was green—green peppermint rice, green parsley bread slices, light green apple cider, apple slices dipped in green whipped cream.

In early England people celebrated the "bringing in the May" on May Day: before dawn, they would go out in the woods and fields to pick flowers and branches to decorate their homes. They also thought that walking barefoot through the morning dew would clean and purify them.

In attempting to make this day Christian, the church adapted many of its rites for the feast of Pentecost, when it became customary to decorate homes with flowers and green branches. The May Queen became the Pentecost Bride, and the notion continues that the dew that falls on Pentecost night has special healing power.

Modern observances of May Day continue. Some colleges still choose their May Queens and hold May dances, ceremonies, and games. In some schools, students erect and dance around Maypoles, while others make May Day baskets. Children fill these baskets with flowers, small gifts, and a doll.

Because of its pagan origin, many countries tried to abolish the ritual of the Maypole but the people simply changed its name. For example, as the Tree of Liberty, it became the symbol of the French Revolution in the seventeenth century.

In the United States, Loyalty Day became the name for May Day. This was celebrated with parades and patriotic addresses given by civic leaders. And in 1961 President Kennedy issued a proclamation to observe May 1 as Law Day. Celebrations developed throughout the country—essays, contests, make-believe trials. All people are asked to look again at the freedom that is ours under the law.

During these first warm days of the year, when the faint smell of green leaves, grass, and warm earth fill our hearts, we become mindful of the call to become alert to God's presence in this season of spring. We welcome the gifts of the spirit within each of us and all creation. In living these gifts for others, we renew the face of the earth.

Preparations

directions

Hang the green panel for the season of spring.

Choose some participants to sound bells, horns, whistles, and so on. Alert them that these will be chimed five times.

Choose three readers.

Place a bowl of water with a sprig of evergreen below the green panel. These will be used for blessing the Maypole and people.

Erect and decorate the Maypole.

Participants are wearing green baldrics. Have names of participants ready for calling.

Optional: Provide green apple cider and green apples (such as Granny Smith) for toasting and welcoming spring.

materials

Bells, horns, whistles, etc.
Bowl of water, evergreen sprig
Green streamers of crepe or material
Paper
Magic markers
Stand and pole

Project

Make, erect, and decorate a Maypole.
Cut out and make flowers, bells, and streamers as decoration.

On the back of some of the flowers and bells, place gifts/fruits of the Spirit (from reading by Reader 3). These will be handed out.

Make and wear green baldrics (streamers cut from crepe or material—see A Background Explanation Reflection).

Prayer Celebration

Opening Greeting

LEADER: We come together to reawaken the spirit of the sleeping earth and the Spirit that dwells deep within our hearts. With the sound of bells, horns, and whistles, we alert the spirits of field and forest as we become aware of the Spirit alive in us.

(Sound bells and other instruments.)

The Readings

LEADER: Let us open our hearts as we welcome the Spirit within us in listening to these words of scripture.

READER 1: "You are like a cedar in Lebanon, with beautiful, shady branches, a tree so tall that it reaches the clouds.
There was water to make it grow, and underground rivers to feed it.
They watered the place where the tree was growing
and sent streams to all the trees of the forest.
Because it was well-watered, it grew taller
    than other trees.
Its branches grew thick and long.
How beautiful the tree was—so tall, with
    such long branches.
Its roots reached down to the deep-flowing
    streams.
No cedar in God's garden could compare with it.
No fir tree ever had such branches, and no plane
    tree such limbs.
No tree in God's own garden was so beautiful
I made it beautiful, with spreading branches.
It was the envy of every tree in the garden
    of God."

Ezekiel 31:3–5, 7–9 GNB (adapted)

This is the Word of the Lord.

ALL: Thanks be to God.

LEADER: Our Maypole represents the cedar tree, a symbol of great strength, beauty, and life.

(sound bells, etc.)

READER 2: "Look at how the wild flowers grow; they do not work or make clothes for themselves. But I tell you that not even King Solomon with all his wealth had clothes as beautiful as one of these flowers. It is God who clothes the wild grass—grass that is here today and gone tomorrow. God will clothe you in the same way."

Matthew 6:28–30 GNB (adapted)

This is the Word of the Lord.

ALL: Thanks be to God.

LEADER: Our flowers decorating our Maypole remind us of God's care and concern for all of us.

(sound bells, etc.)

The green we wear speaks of our welcome to the spring greening of the earth and the newness of life in us.

(sound bells, etc.)

And as the May dew was once used to cleanse and purify, so we sprinkle with water our May Pole and each of us with newness.

(sound bells, etc.)

In newness, we listen to these words from scripture. They invite us to live in a new way in the life of the Spirit.

READER 3: "Let the Spirit lead you. Let the Spirit produce in you love, joy, peace, patience, kindness, goodness, faithfulness, humility, self-control (gentleness, knowledge, endurance, wisdom, understanding, courage). The Spirit has given us life. Plant yourself in the field of the Spirit and from the Spirit you will have life."

Galatians 5:22–25, 6:8 (adapted)

This is the Word of the Lord.

ALL: Thanks be to God.

LEADER: As I call your name, come forward and receive a gift of the Spirit.
____(Name)____, I invite you to receive the gift of _____.

(Bell or flower with name of gift is given.)

Think for a moment of the way in which you can give this gift to others.

(pause)

On your baldric, place the flower or bell sign of your gift.

(pause)

As the Spirit reawakens life within us, so we share this reawakening with all creation.

Circling the Maypole

LEADER: As people have for centuries, we sing and dance around our gaily decorated Maypole, in celebration of May. With hearts filled with gratitude and thanksgiving for the awakened Spirit within us, we show our joy as we move in a circle around our Maypole and sing (to tune of "Here We Go Round the Mulberry Bush"),

ALL: Here we go round the merry Maypole,
The merry Maypole, the merry Maypole,
Here we go round the merry Maypole
On a cold and fresh May morning.

(Circle stops but participants continue singing, making appropriate actions to the following verses.)

This is the way we bring in the May . . . (etc.)

(Bend to pick flowers and reach to cut branches.)

This is the way we gather May dew...(etc.)

(Gather and rub on face.)

This is the way we stamp for spring . . . (etc.)

(Lift right foot and stamp down.)

Closing Blessing

LEADER: Our response will be: "Lord, send us in your Spirit and we will renew the face of the earth." In the gift of faith,

ALL: Lord, send us in your Spirit and we will renew the face of the earth.

LEADER: In the gift of hope,

ALL: Lord, send us in your Spirit and we will renew the face of the earth.

LEADER: In the gift of love,

ALL: Lord, send us in your Spirit and we will renew the face of the earth.

LEADER: May almighty God, bless you, the Father, and the Son, and the Holy Spirit.

ALL: Amen.

(Optional: Toast each other with green apple cider or eat green apples to welcome spring.)

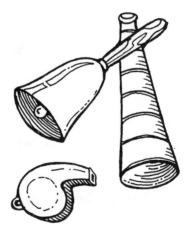

Ascension Day

A Background Reflection

Ascension Day celebrates Jesus' ascent into heaven after rising from the dead. The earliest recorded observance of this feast of the Ascension was in the fourth century A.D. when it was commemorated and celebrated forty days after Easter. John Chrysostom refers to Ascension Day as an "ancient and universal" festival, and Augustine claims it originated with the apostles. Scripture tells us that Jesus "was lifted up before their eyes, and a cloud took him out of their sight" (Acts 1:9). At his Father's side, Jesus continues to pour out his spirit so that, commissioned in his love, we the people can continue to do his work in our own lives.

In medieval European villages, torches and colorful banners were carried in procession through the streets. Wells were blessed and the trellises over them were decorated with flowers. In England, the people walked the boundaries of their parishes and placed wreaths on stone property markers. The parish priest offered God's blessing for the crops. In some countries herbs and teas were gathered; there was a belief that a drink from seven kinds of herbs gave a person immunity from contagious diseases.

Since a cloud received Jesus, Ascension Day became a time for weather predictions in many places. Clouds have often been a sign of God's presence in scripture: "A cloud followed them by day to show them the way" (Exodus 13:21), and "Out of the cloud came a voice that said, 'This is my beloved son. Listen to him'" (Matthew 17:5). The cloud is also an allusion to Christ at the final coming and a prelude to the coming of the Spirit.

Perhaps we should extend those cloud-gazing moments of our youth into our adult world. Gazing at clouds can give us a meditative moment of quiet and prayer as we use our imagination to picture the delights and beauty of God's world. Living in time and space, the cloud can be welcomed as a symbol of God, as it is in scripture.

Sewing, sweeping, and working on Ascension Day were thought to bring ill fortune to the home for the remaining year. This Sabbath notion of no work on a holy day can be a sign of our anticipation of the kingdom. Instead of a work day, Ascension Day became a traditional day for mountain climbing and picnics on hilltops where cloud gazing can be done leisurely and with no distractions.

In the Western church, Ascension Day inaugurates the eight days of Ascensiontide, which last to the eve of Pentecost. In some churches the paschal candle, lighted on the eve of Easter as a symbol of the resurrected Christ, is extinguished on Ascension Day as a sign that the Light of the Word is no longer with us in his bodily presence as he once was. Rather, as the Body of Christ, the people are invited to be his light to others.

Ephesians 3:10 says that Jesus "ascended far above the heavens so that he might fill all things." The commissioning and blessing given to the disciples to preach the good news is ours also. Like the disciples, we are found together as a people of God bringing and living good news to the four corners of the earth, working for peace and justice for all men and women. While bodily presence calls attention to one place, one geographical location, the Ascension tells us of spiritual and universal presence to all people across the globe. And we are never alone, for the man Jesus who lived among us, who ate and walked with us, even though he died, is living and present among us and within us.

Preparations

directions

Hang the green panel for the season of spring. Place a candle before the panel. If using a Yule Wheel, place a candle in the center. Use four other candles on the wheel for north, south, east, west.

Choose participants to be the different people and props in the story: a mountain, a cloud, Jesus, eleven disciples (designate three for east, three for west, three for north, two for south), and alert them to the words they will be saying.

Place signs for north, south, east and west in four areas.

Prepare singing.

Choose participants for playing the drum, tambourine, and so on. Let them become familiar with the times to do so.

materials

Candles,
Drum, tambourine, etc.
Poster board, paper
Magic markers
Scissors

disciple

Jesus

mountain

cloud

Prayer Celebration

Opening Greeting

LEADER: We gather to renew our hearts and spirits as together we celebrate the promise of Jesus to be with us in all that we do. Forty days have passed since Jesus rose from the dead. During this time Jesus helps the people deepen their belief in him. But now he must return to his father.

As we light this Christ candle, we remember that what Jesus did and said as he lived among us.

(Pause and light center candle.)

Together we become a part of the story of Jesus as we listen to what happened on Ascension Day.

A Scripture Presentation

(adapted and based on Matthew 28:16–20)

LEADER: There was a mountain in Galilee.

(Mountain actor appears; sound instruments.)

And to this mountain, Jesus summoned the eleven disciples. "Come this way. Come."

(Jesus gestures.)

The eleven disciples made their way up the mountain.

(eleven drum strokes as the eleven march in place)

When they saw Jesus, they fell down in homage.

(Disciples kneel and bow.)

And Jesus came forward and said,

JESUS: Full authority has been given me. Go and make disciples of all nations. Baptize them in the name of the Father and of the Son and of the Holy Spirit.

Go to the east.

(Three disciples go to the east station and say as they make the sign of the cross:)

EAST VOICES: We baptize you in the name of the Father and of the Son and of the Holy Spirit.

JESUS: Go to the west.

(Another group goes to the west station and say as they make the sign of the cross:)

WEST VOICES: We baptize you in the name of the Father and of the Son and of the Holy Spirit.

JESUS: Go to the south.

(Another group goes to the south station and say as they make the sign of the cross:)

SOUTH VOICES: We baptize you in the name of the Father and of the Son and of the Holy Spirit.

JESUS: Go to the north.

(Another group goes to the north station and say as they make the sign of the cross:)

NORTH VOICES: We baptize you in the name of the Father and of the Son and of the Holy Spirit.

JESUS: Teach them to carry out everything I have commanded you, to do my work. And disciples of the east, proclaim to everyone: Carry out the work of love.

EAST VOICES: Carry out the work of love.

ALL: We will. We will.

JESUS: And disciples of the west, proclaim to everyone: Carry out the work of caring for others.

WEST VOICES: Carry out the work of caring for others.

ALL: We will. We will.

JESUS: And disciples of the south, proclaim to everyone: Carry out the work of being kind.

SOUTH VOICES: Carry out the work of being kind.

ALL: We will. We will.

JESUS: And disciples of the north, proclaim to everyone: Carry out the work of helping others.

NORTH VOICES: Carry out the work of helping others.

ALL: We will. We will.

JESUS: And know that I am with you always, until the end of the world.

(Cloud appears and slowly moves in front of Jesus. Everyone looks up and sings to the tune of "Angels Watching Over Me.")

ALL: All night, all day,
Working for the Lord we are, we are,
All night, all day,
Working for the Lord, we are.

Psalm Response

LEADER: Men and women of ___(place)___ why were you looking up into the sky?
This Jesus who has been taken up will return.
Let our response to our psalm of praise be
"Alleluia! Alleluia!"
God ascends to shouts of joy!

ALL: Alleluia! Alleulia!

LEADER: The Lord ascends to the blast of trumpets!

ALL: Alleluia! Alleulia!

LEADER: All you people clap your hands!

ALL: Alleluia! Alleulia!

LEADER: Shout to God with cries of gladness!

ALL: Alleluia! Alleulia!

LEADER: For the Lord, the most high, the Awesome one is the King over all the earth.

ALL: Alleluia! Alleulia!

LEADER: Sing praise to God, sing praise, sing praise to our king.

ALL: Alleluia! Alleulia!

LEADER: God reigns over all the nations. Sing hymns of praise.

ALL: Alleluia! Alleulia!

Psalm 47 (adapted)

Closing Blessing

LEADER: From this Christ candle we light the candles of east, west, north, and south. We extinguish the Christ candle as a sign that the Light of the World is no longer with us as he once was. Jesus invites us to be his light to others. As we look at these lights, we renew in our hearts the commission of Jesus to continue his work. We become Jesus for others and receive Jesus from others as the body of Christ. Bow your heads for God's blessing: Lord, may we follow you into the new creation. Give us voices that speak,

ALL: Give us voices that speak,

LEADER: Hands that work,

ALL: Hands that work,

LEADER: Feet that journey,

ALL: Feet that journey,

LEADER: And eyes that gaze at the splendor of your world,

ALL: And eyes that gaze at the splendor of your world.

LEADER: Your ascension, Lord, is our glory and our hope!

ALL: Alleluia! Alleulia! Alleluia!

LEADER: In the name of the Father, and of the Son, and of the Holy Spirit.

ALL: Amen.

Trinity Sunday

A Background Reflection

Trinity Sunday celebrates the fundamental Christian belief of one God in three persons. The word *Trinity* was first used by second-century Christians to express this belief in one word. During the fourth century, belief in the Trinity was beautifully expressed ritually in the home by lighting the evening lamps and saying the words "We praise the Father, Son, and Holy Spirit." It was also during the fourth century that belief in the Trinity was finally expressed in the Nicene creed.

In a prayer of praise, the doxology, we express our belief in the mystery of the Trinity. This ancient Christian doxology came into the Western church by the fifth century. The first part of the prayer—"Glory to the Father, Son, and Holy Spirit"—was used in the Eastern church. The second part—"As it was in the beginning, is now, and ever shall be, world without end"—was added during the reign of Constantine. The Liturgy of the Hours uses this prayer throughout; one is invited to bow in reverence as the first part is said. Francis of Assisi recommended constant repetition of this doxology daily as a centering help to spirituality.

In the Sign of the Cross, the earliest Christians professed belief in the Trinity and in Jesus as healer and redeemer. During the time of Augustine, people made the sign of the cross with three fingers on their foreheads without any words. This three-finger cross on the forehead was used before all undertakings—upon entering and leaving a place, before eating, dressing, sleeping, before reading, writing, and each new task. It alerts us to the presence of God in all that we do. Today many people make the Sign of the Cross to begin community or private prayer.

Many symbolic pictures and designs have been used to try and express this mystery of faith. We are familiar with the folklore about St. Patrick of Ireland using the symbol of the trefoil or shamrock. The pansy, once called the Trinity flower and one of the oldest perennial garden flowers, has three petals that overlap and that expressed for many the image of the Trinity. Some people joined three tapers together at their base and then lit them to express this three-in-one belief. Paintings from the first centuries show the Trinity represented by three young men of identical shape and looks. Much later in European wayside shrines, churches, and homes, the figure of a triangle surrounded by rays with a picture of an eye inside (symbol of God's constant love and protection) could be found. North American folk art depicts the Trinity as present in the heart of a person. Inside this drawn heart sits the Father and Son with the dove between them.

During the seventeenth and eighteenth centuries, public columns of marble or granite were erected in honor of the Trinity throughout central Europe. On the feast of the Trinity, people would gather for festive and joyful celebrations in the city squares before these columns. Devotion to the Trinity flourished at this time.

Many explanations for the Trinity have been attempted. One interpretation, "Light of sun, light of moon, and light of air in nature and substance are the same light and yet are three distinct lights." An explanation from the American Indians says, "Go down to the river in winter, dig through snow and come to ice. Chop through ice and come to water. Snow is water, ice is water, water is water, and all three are one."

As mystery, the Trinity can never be fully understood. But as a sign of mutuality and oneness, this model of Trinity invites us to live in peace, harmony, and love with one another. Paul called on the Trinity as he greeted the arguing Corinthians and apostles in a plea for peace (2 Corinthians 13:11–13). The whole of creation is an expression of the community, the unity in love, among the persons of the Trinity. As creation we are invited to create a communion among people on earth in the likeness of the communion among the persons of the Trinity. We feel empowered to do this with the praying words of Jesus: "May they be one in us just as you are in me, and I am in you" (John 17:21).

Preparations

directions

Hang the green panel (for the season of spring), which has been made into a Trinity column.

Choose five readers.

Explain the gesture of bowing to the words "Glory be to the Father and the Son and the Holy Spirit."

Remind participants of the invitation during the prayer service of speaking their own beliefs from their project.

Ask participants to place the pansy they will receive in their homes or room during this Trinity season. Have ready a list of their names for calling them forth.

materials

Paper/pens/pencils
Pins
Scissors
Green spring panel

Project

Make a Trinity column. With wire, form a circle and attach the green material for spring. Hang the circle from ceiling.

Make pansy petals. Participants are invited to write or draw what they believe about God, Jesus, the Spirit, themselves, creation, the Church, and so on in composing their own personal creed. Each belief is put on a pansy petal. Groups of three petals, a trefoil sign of the Trinity, are then pinned on the Trinity column.

Make a pansy for each participant with his or her name on it. These pansies will be given to each participant during the prayer celebration.

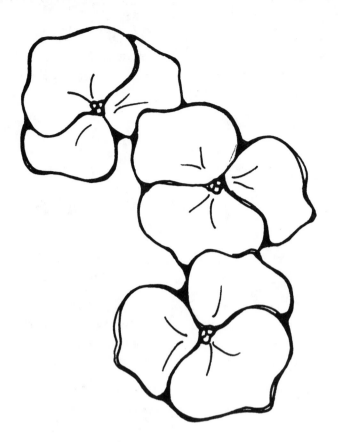

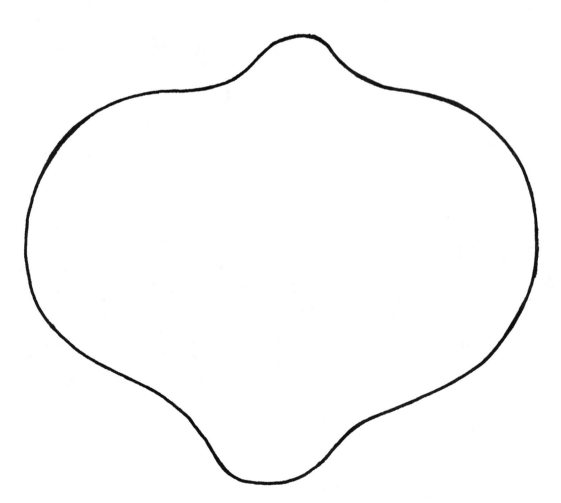

Prayer Celebration

Opening Greeting

LEADER: We honor the mystery of the Trinity in our life as we give glory, power and joyful praise forever and ever. As a sign of our belief, we make the Sign of the Cross:

(do so and say:)

ALL: In the name of the Father, and of the Son, and of the Holy Spirit. Amen.

The Readings

LEADER: Let us listen to the words of scripture as Jesus speaks in prayer to his father and in love to us, his friends.

READER 1: And Jesus speaks in prayer to his father:
"I Pray that they may all be one, Father. May they be one in us, just as you are in me and I in you. May they be one, just as you and I are one."

John 17:20–22 (adapted)

This is the Word of the Lord.

ALL: Thanks be to God.

LEADER: We show a sign of this oneness by gathering in a circle around our Trinity column.

(pause)

READER 2: And Jesus speaks in love to his friends:
"I have much more to tell you but now it would be too much for you to bear. When, however, the Spirit comes, who reveals the truth about God, the Spirit will lead you. All that my Father has is mine; that is why I said that the Spirit will take what I give and tell it to you."

John 16:12–15 (adapted)

This is the Word of the Lord.

ALL: Thanks be to God.

LEADER: Each of the pansies on our column speaks of the way we have listened to the Spirit in our life, of the way we have been led by the Spirit in what we believe. As we are called by name, we come forth to receive our own name pansy as a sign of the presence of the Trinity within each of us.

    _____(Name)_____, live the life of the Father, Son, and Holy Spirit.

(With three fingers, sign the cross on the forehead of each participant.)

Profession of Faith

LEADER: Let us profess our faith by naming the way we experience God in our life.

READER 3: We name God, *Father.*
We believe in God, the Father almighty
    the one who made all things,
    the one who continues to give life and being to all,
    the one who is.

LEADER: We bow and say,

(All bow.)

ALL: Glory be to the Father, and to the Son, and to the Holy Spirit.

READER 4: We name God, *Son.*
We believe in the Son
the one made man in Jesus,
the one who taught us of the
Father's love,
the one who died and rose.

LEADER: We bow and say,

(All bow.)

ALL: Glory be to the Father, and to the Son, and to the Holy Spirit.

READER 5: We name God, *Spirit.*
We believe in the Holy spirit
the one promised by Jesus
the one who is with us always,
the one who is lovingly
present in each person
and in the community called
church.

LEADER: We bow and say,

(All bow.)

ALL: Glory be to the Father, and to the Son, and to the Holy Spirit.

LEADER: Our Trinity column holds our own personal beliefs and signs of the way in which we experience God daily in our life. And so we say,

(Invite individual participants to share their beliefs.)

ALL: We believe . . . .

LEADER: We bow and say,

(All bow.)

ALL: Glory be to the Father, and to the Son, and to the Holy Spirit. Amen.

Closing Blessing

LEADER: We are greeted and sent forth in the words of Paul to the Corinthians. To each of these sendings, we respond, "Amen." And now my brothers and sisters, goodbye. Strive for perfection. Be good listeners.

ALL: Amen.

LEADER: Agree with one another. Live in peace.

ALL: Amen.

LEADER: Greet others in kindness and gentleness. Build up the Spirit of everyone you meet.

ALL: Amen.

LEADER: All of God's people send you their blessing. And may the grace of the Lord Jesus Christ, the love of God and the fellowship of the Holy Spirit be with you all.

ALL: And also with you.

2 Corinthians 13:11–13 (adapted)

Midsummer's Eve

A Background Reflection

Sometimes a holiday is not what it says it is. For example, Midsummer is a holiday celebrated not in the middle of summertime, as its name would suggest, but at summer's beginning. Midsummer commemorates the summer solstice as the sun seems to stand still and our days are longest and nights shortest. It is a festival to honor the sun and the earth's awakening after the winter's sleep. In his play *A Midsummer Night's Dream*, Shakespeare reflects the foolishness and spirit of the night in love matching and in using divinations to foretell the future and discover the identity of the one who loves you.

In one rite, people exchanged pots of basil or marjoram while singing around the fire:

St. John, St. John,
Don't let this summer pass
Give me a sweetheart, St. John,
A sweetheart, a sweetheart,
For I would wed.

For centuries Midsummer was an important festival in many countries. Fire would blaze on mountaintops and along shores. Bonfires were thought to purity air and water and drive away evil from the land. Midsummer's Eve was the shortest night of the year, and people would stay up all night dancing around the fires, then greeting and drinking a toast to the morning sun.

The sun was worshiped in the symbolism of fire. Wreaths of certain herbs were thrown into the fire, and their singed remains were brought home to protect households. Sometimes thistles, symbolic of the sun, were gathered and (with fir branches) placed on barns, in fields, or homes as protection against the power of darkness.

In some countries, it was customary to float lighted candles on water. If your small candle boat safely sailed from shore to shore, then you would have good luck for the coming year. Festival fires on water were thought to foretell the future. The sails of fishing vessels were colorfully decorated, churches embroidered and displayed colored banners, and the people saluted one another in the "kiss of peace"—a peace offering for the future.

While people were waiting and longing for summer, John the Baptist proclaimed that they need wait no longer, for the Light had come into the world. It is interesting that the early church chose this ancient feast of the sun to celebrate the birthday of John the Baptist, adding simple water rites to purify this pagan observance. Augustine speaks of John as representing times past and as being the herald of things to come. Scripture tells us that John "came to bear witness to the light, to prepare an upright people for the Lord" (Luke 1:11). John preached the arrival of the Messiah and the change of heart necessary in recognizing the nearness of the Kingdom.

Light is needed for this recognition, needed to see below the surface of life and to look carefully at our lives and values. Jesus is the Light. But as "bearing witness to the Light," John is like the sun described in Genesis. Here the sun is referred to as a creature of God (Yahweh), created after light, and moving in obedience to God. John, too, moves in obedience to God—as God's prophet. And as prophet he does more than foretell the future, as the pagan rites of Midsummer sought to do, but rather points clearly to the signs already present, that God has visited the people in Jesus, the Light.

In medieval Europe, a procession dance called Threading the Needle closed the Midsummer festival. Guests were invited to hold candles or green boughs in hand and rotate clockwise around the fire in imitation of the path of the sun rising in the east and setting in the west. Two people with raised arms form an arch—the Needle's Eye—and the guests pass under their arch as the thread. The threaded needle is now ready "to sew the year's traditions to life."

Preparations

directions

Hang the yellow panel for the season of summer.

Choose two readers.

Form a circle with candles. (If you have a Yule Wheel, you may want to use it.) Place fir greens or birch leaves in the center of the circle. Place before the yellow panel.

For sprinkling and blessing, have a bowl of water and evergreen sprig.

Hang colored ribbons with a thistle around circle.

Acquaint participants with the process of Threading the Needle. Choose two people to form the arch for Threading the Needle at the end of the ceremony.

Remind participants that they will be invited to share the message blessing from the ribbon they choose during prayer service

materials

Yellow panel for spring
Colored ribbon (fabric or paper)
Candles and holders (Yule Wheel optional)
Greens or birch leaves
Crayons, magic markers
Scissors
Glue
Bowl of water, fir sprig

Project

Cut out 2- x 4-inch ribbons from colored fabric, or use crepe paper streamers. Choose sun colors of yellow, orange, red.

Cut out thistles (or if real thistles are available, gather them). Place a thistle on each ribbon.

On back of each ribbon, have participants choose and write one of the following message blessings or create one of their own. These can be taken after the prayer service. Suggested message blessings are "a gentle spirit," "patience and hope," "life and love," "good health," "peace and joy," "protection from all fears," "a cheerful heart," and so on.

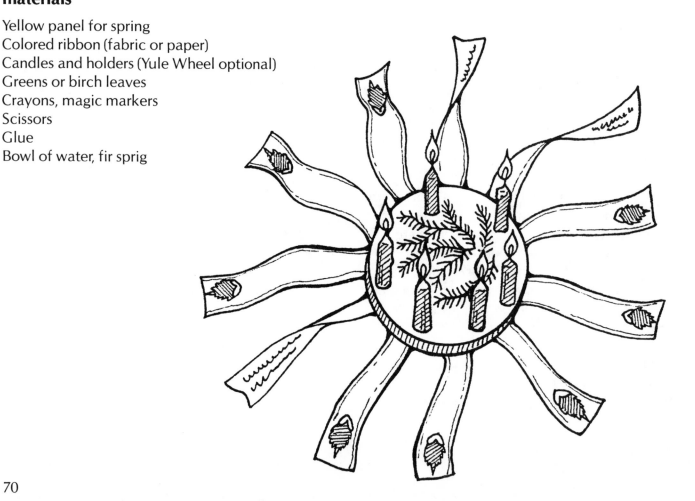

Prayer Celebration

Opening Greeting

LEADER: As the morning sun helps us to greet the newness of the day, so in light we recognize the nearness of God in our life. Let us join together to celebrate Midsummer's Eve, our longest day of light. We bring our hands together and bow in greeting to this sun's light, which the Lord has made.

(pause)

Lighting of the Sun Candle

LEADER: We light this circle of candles, representative of the sun. We remember from the creation story that "God made the sun and placed it in the sky to rule over the day. And God was pleased with what had been made"

Genesis 1:16–18 (adapted)

(pause)

Take a moment to recall in your own life a time of appreciation for this sun gift.

(pause)

For the brightness of day, we give thanks for what you have made, Lord.

ALL: We give thanks for what you have made, Lord.

LEADER: For the light that warms the earth, we give thanks for what you have made, Lord.

ALL: We give thanks for what you have made, Lord.

LEADER: For the sun's rays helping all things to grow, we give thanks for what you have made, Lord.

ALL: We give thanks for what you have made, Lord.

LEADER: With the light of understanding, let us listen to this psalm reading from scripture.

READER 1: "How clearly the sky reveals God's glory. How plainly it shows what God has done. Each day announces it to the following day; each night repeats it to the next. No speech or words are used, no sound is heard, yet their message goes out to all the world and is heard to the ends of the earth. God made a home in the sky for the sun; it comes out in the morning like a happy bridegroom, like an athlete eager to run a race. It starts at one end of the sky and goes across to the other. Nothing can hide from its heat."

Psalm 19:1–6 GNB

This is the Word of the Lord.

ALL: Thanks be to God.

A Water Blessing

LEADER: On Midsummer's Eve we celebrate the birthday of John the Baptist. Although he himself is not the light, John comes to speak about and point out the long-awaited light of the world, Jesus.

READER 2: "Do not be afraid, Zechariah. God has heard your prayer, and your wife Elizabeth will bear you a son. You are to name him John. How glad and happy you will be, and how happy many others will be when he is born. He will be a great man in the Lord's sight. He must not drink any wine or strong drink. From his very birth he will be filled with the Holy Spirit and he will bring back many of the people of Israel to the Lord. He will go ahead of the Lord, strong and mighty like the prophet Elijah. He will bring fathers and children together again; he will turn disobedient people back to the way of thinking of the righteous; he will get the Lord's people ready."

Luke 1:13–17 GNB

This is the Word of the Lord.

ALL: Thanks be to God.

LEADER: With water, we sprinkle and bless our sun circle and greens,

(pause)

and we bless all people present,

(pause)

for together with the gift of sun and earth, we make ready for Jesus daily in our hearts.

Presentation

LEADER: Each of our sun rays holds a word of blessing for the home. A thistle, symbolic of the sun, adorns each ray. Together, let us choose one of these rays,

(pause)

and now share the blessing we have received.

(Call participants by name.)

_____(Name)_____,
what blessing will you bring to your home?

PARTICIPANT: I will bring to my home a blessing of (response of participant).

LEADER: We thank God for the birth of John the Baptist and for the way he helped us to recognize Jesus as the light of our homes.

Closing Blessing

LEADER: Holding our ray blessing and in silence, we move around our circle sun in imitation of the path of the sun rising in the east and setting in the west.

(pause)

We carry home our ray blessing to place it on a doorway of our home. Let us bow our heads to God's blessing. Our response will be "Amen."
May God's light rise on you like the sun.

ALL: Amen.

LEADER: May God's compassion shine on you like the dawn.

ALL: Amen.

LEADER: May God's mercy brighten your walkways like the noonday sun.

ALL: Amen.

LEADER: And in the evening twilight, may you know the warmth and gentleness of God's love for you.

ALL: Amen.

LEADER: As a threaded needle sews the traditions of our life together, may we now go forth as thread through the needle's eye to live in the light for others.

(Participants form a serpentine line and move through the arch formed by the raised arms of two people.)

Swithin's Day

A Background Reflection

July celebrates summer's abundance of fruits, vegetables, outdoor pleasures—and rain. England offers us St. Swithin's Day, where we are invited to celebrate a charming weather holiday. It is said that if it rains on Swithin's Day the next forty days will also be rainy. If it is dry on Swithin's Day, forty days of drought will follow. Folklore also proclaims that apples watered by this day's rain become especially luscious.

Eating symbolic foods offers us a way to celebrate and reflect on the meaning of a holiday. Long ago on Swithin's Day, large apples were polished and cut in half horizontally. With this cut, the seeds appear to be arranged in a star shape called a *pentagle*. The five-sided continuous design represented the perfection of the cycle of the year having no beginning or end. The cut apple is dipped in water and eaten. The water is said to represent the tears of St. Swithin, while the apple's pentagle represents timelessness.

St. Swithin was a bishop in England in the ninth century A.D. Educated as a teacher, he was an advisor to the king in the arts and religious matters. He built and repaired churches and was known to the village people for his humility and his charity to the poor. Being a humble man, he had asked, so the legend goes, to be buried outside Winchester Cathedral, under the eaves, where he would be closer to the working people of Winchester as they passed by than if he had been buried inside.

Upon his death, the request was granted. One hundred years later, according to the legend, the monks decided that this lowly grave under the dripping eaves was not a suitable resting place for so great a man and that he should be moved inside the church. The faithful townspeople felt this would be against Swithin's wishes.

Nevertheless, a great assembly of clergy gathered with much pomp and ceremony on the appointed transfer day. At the moment the ceremony began, down from the sky poured a tremendous rainstorm. It rained steadily for forty days and nights. The deluge simply reinforced what the townspeople believed all along—that Swithin did not wish to be removed!

Ever after, the rain or fair of St. Swithin's Day was thought to predict the weather. Country folk chanted a rhyme:

> St. Swithin's Day, if it does rain
> For forty days it will remain.
> St. Swithin's Day, if it is fair
> For forty days, t'will rain no more.

One is reminded of the weather forecast offered Noah and his family. God told Noah that it would rain forty days and forty nights. Trusting in this forecast, Noah listened to God's instructions to build an ark and gather animals, two of every kind, as well as his whole family, into the ark. Indeed, the rain came down for forty days and nights. Finally, when the dove he sent out returned with an olive branch in her beak, Noah knew that the waters of the deluge had started to recede. On reaching land, Noah and his family immediately built an altar and gave thanks to God. The sign of the rainbow after the rain is God's promise to be with us forever.

The timelessness of the story of Noah and the legend of St. Swithin call us to touch the timelessness of God within and among us. In Noah's sign of the rainbow, let us recognize our oneness in the Spirit and confirm the promise of God to be with us always.

Preparations

directions

Hang the yellow panel for the season of summer. Place a rainbow on this panel.

Be prepared to place the number 40 on this panel during ceremony.

Place a table for Noah's altar before the panel. On the table, put horizontally cut apples and a bowl of water. These will be passed around during the ceremony.

Choose participants for different roles in the story of Noah: God, Noah, two dogs, two birds, two donkeys, two goats, two mice, one dove. These all have speaking roles. All remaining participants become Noah's wife, sons and daughters, wives and husbands.

Define the space for the ark and explain that they will be called into that space as their character. Practice the sounds that animals will make.

Each participant should have a decorated piece of paper with his or her name on it.

Be prepared to call each person by name.

materials

Yellow panel
Table
Apples, bowl of water
Colored paper of yellow, green, red, orange, blue, indigo, purple, white
Magic markers
Scissors
Pins or tape

Project

Make the number 40 (draw or cut).

Make a rainbow from the colored paper.

From a chosen rainbow color, each participant makes and decorates his or her name. These will be placed on the rainbow during ceremony.

Have participants make a sign for the character they are portraying in story of Noah.

Prayer Celebration

Opening Greeting

LEADER: July celebrates summer and the abundance of fruits, vegetables, outdoor fun—and rain. On this weather holiday of St. Swithin, we are invited to remember that farmers need weather predictions for planting and harvesting. In the words and folklore of long ago, we chant the rhyme of forecasting the weather:
"St. Swithin's Day if it does rain,"

ALL: St. Swithin's Day if it does rain,

LEADER: "For forty days it will remain."

ALL: For forty days it will remain.

LEADER: "St. Swithin's Day, if it is fair,"

ALL: St. Swithin's Day, if it is fair,

LEADER: "For forty days t'will rain no more."

ALL: For forty days t'will rain no more.

LEADER: On this day we remember also the scripture story of the Flood, where Noah was given a similar weather forecast—rain for forty days and forty nights. On our banner we place the number 40.

(pause)

On our altar, we place our cut apples. Apples from trees watered by the rain of St. Swithin's Day were always thought to be the most delicious and most nourishing.

(pause)

Rainbow Presentation

LEADER: Many times after a rain, a bow of light appears in the sky. The rainbow is a natural sign of God's presence in our life. The colors red, orange, yellow, green, blue, indigo, and purple are on our rainbow. On our chosen colors, we place our names. Our names are signs of our uniqueness as persons and represents the individual gifts that are ours.

(Call names and present name papers.)

However, as the rainbow is one, so are we one in the Spirit, each sharing and living our gifts in the service of others. May we let rainbows confirm the promise of God with us always.

The Story of Noah

LEADER: This is the story of the ark, a story of Noah, his wife, his family, and the animals who went into the ark for forty days and forty nights because of God's love and care for them.

GOD: "Noah, you are a good and faithful man. I say to you and your family, Build a boat out of good timber.

(Noah builds.)

Build it with three decks.

(Noah builds.)

Build it with a door on the side.

(Noah builds.)

I am going to send a flood on the earth. Now call into the boat two birds and animals of every kind."

NOAH: Come, dogs.

(Dogs bark.)

Come, birds.

(Birds sing.)

Come, donkeys.

(Donkeys bray.)

Come, goats.

(Goats bleat.)

Come, mice.

(Mice squeak.)

Come, dove.

(Dove coos.)

Come, my wife, sons, and daughters, and your wives, husbands, and children.

LEADER: And the rain began to fall. The floodgates of the sky were opened and the rain fell, and it rained and rained and rained. For forty days and nights it rained.

ALL: And it rained and rained and rained. For forty days and nights it rained.

LEADER: And while it rained, a flood covered the earth, covered even the mountains on the earth. And the dogs said this prayer:

DOGS: "Lord, we keep watch. If we are not here, who will guard, who will be faithful? No one but you and us understand what faithfulness is. Lord, let us always keep watch for you."

LEADER: And it rained and rained and rained. For forty days and nights it rained.

ALL: And it rained and rained and rained. For forty days and nights it rained.

LEADER: And the little birds said this prayer:

BIRDS: "Dear God, we don't know how to pray by ourselves very well. Please protect our nest from wind and rain and set our hearts with music so we can sing of you for others. Please, Lord."

LEADER: And it rained and rained and rained. For forty days and nights it rained.

ALL: And it rained and rained and rained. For forty days and nights it rained.

LEADER: And the donkeys said this prayer:

DONKEYS: "O, God, you made us to trudge along the road and to carry heavy loads. Give us courage and gentleness. One day, let somebody understand us. Let us find a juicy thistle and make them give us time to eat it for our lunch."

LEADER: And it rained and rained and rained. For forty days and nights it rained.

ALL: And it rained and rained and rained. For forty days and nights it rained.

LEADER: And the goats said this prayer:

GOATS: "Lord, let us live as we will. We need freedom, and a little giddiness of the heart. The sheep do not understand, for they all graze in the same direction. But we, we love to leap with our hearts to all your marvels."

LEADER: And it rained and rained and rained. For forty days and nights it rained.

ALL: And it rained and rained and rained. For forty days and nights it rained.

LEADER: And the mice said this prayer:

MICE: "Dear God, we are so little and gray, how can you keep us in mind? Nobody ever gives us anything, and we nibble for food. Who made us but you? Let us stay hidden with you always."

LEADER: And it rained and rained and rained. For forty days and nights it rained.

ALL: And it rained and rained and rained. For forty days and nights it rained.

LEADER: And the dove said this prayer:

DOVE: "Lord, the ark waits on your will and is the sign of your peace. I am the dove, simple as the sweetness that comes from you. The ark waits, Lord; it has endured. Let me carry it a sprig of hope and joy."

LEADER: And suddenly the rain stopped. And Noah sent the dove to see if there was dry land. And the dove returned in the evening with a fresh olive branch in its beak. Noan opened the door of the boat. He saw that the ground was dry. And the voice of God was heard:

GOD: "Come out of the ark and form a circle of thanksgiving — you, Noah, your wife, your sons and daughters and their wives and husbands. Come out of the ark, all you animals. I give you this earth.

(Animals come forth as names are called, make their sound, and form a circle before rainbow.)

Come, dogs.

(sound)

Come, birds.

(sound)

Come, donkeys.

(sound)

Come, goats.

(sound)

Come, mice.

(sound)

Come, dove.

(sound)

LEADER: And everyone together said, "Give thanks, for God is good. God's love is everlasting."

ALL: Give thanks, for God is good. God's love is everlasting.

LEADER: Before his altar that Noah built, his family and all the birds and animals bowed.

(pause and do so)

And they heard the voice of God:

GOD: "I am now making my covenant with you and with your descendants and with all living beings, all animals and birds. I promise that never again will water cover the earth. As long as the world exists, there will be a time for planting, and a time for harvest. There will always be cold and heat, summer and winter, day and night. As a sign of this covenant, I will set my rainbow in the sky. The rainbow will be a sign of my presence to be with you always."

Genesis 8:22, 9:10, 12, 13 (adapted)

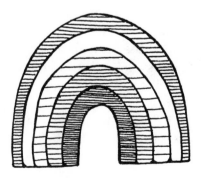

Closing Rite of Timelessness

LEADER: Take a slice of apple and dip it into the water as it is passed. The inside continuous design of our apple represents the cycle of the year. The seeds arranged, as if in a star, speak of timelessness. As we dip our apples in the water, we remember and confirm God's promise to be with us always.

(Pause and dip apples.)

As we eat our apples, we confirm our promise to be faithful to God throughout all the moments of our life— through seedtime and harvest, day and night.

(Pause and eat apples.)

Let us bow our heads for God's blessing. Go forth, one in the Spirit.

ALL: Amen.

LEADER: Live your gifts in the service of others.

ALL: Amen.

LEADER: In the sign of the rainbow, remember the promise of God to be with you always.

ALL: Amen.

LEADER: And may God the Father, and the Son, and the Holy Spirit bless you forever.

ALL: Amen.

Lammas Day

A Background Reflection

August is bread time; it is spring's promise fulfilled. Celebrated long ago as a harvest feast, this first day of August was called Lammas ("loaf mass") from the custom of presenting in church a loaf of wheat bread as an offering of the first fruits of the harvest. Grains and breads were blessed, and thanks were offered to God for a good harvest.

Needless to say, breads were important in this festival for the menu and decorations of the medieval halls. A bread castle was raised on a platform in the middle of the room and eaten at the end of the evening. Bread courses were served: currant buns, shortbread, gingerbread, cucumber bread, and plum bread. A favorite Lammas drink was Lamb's Wool, a splendid warm spiced cider with frothy baked apples floating on top.

The last event in the medieval Lammas Feast was a candlelight procession around the hall. Everyone present held a small loaf of bread with a candle set into it. Guests circled the hall three times. Each participant held the bread that would be eaten in his or her home the following day—with the exception of one quarter. That quarter would be carefully preserved until next Lammas Day, when it would be crumbled to feed the birds.

In both the Hebrew and Christian scriptures, bread is the staple diet, the staff of life. Common bread was made of barley flour; wheat bread was a luxury. Bread was baked daily, leavened or unleavened. Unleavened bread was made when the Jewish people fled from Egypt, and the feast of Passover continues to celebrate this Exodus event with *matza*, unleavened bread. In the Christian scriptures, the term *bread* refers to little flat loaves (Matthew 4:3, 7:9 Lk. 4:3), made of wheat or barley—much like Lebanese or Syrian (pita) bread today. No meal was without bread, for it was the primary food and three loaves usually sufficed for a meal.

Jesus, alluding to the Eucharist, called himself the living bread that comes down from heaven (John 6:32, 51). Partaking of the Eucharist symbolizes the unity of Christians in one bread and one body.

Jesus is often associated with bread as a symbol. Two disciples "knew Jesus in the breaking of the bread," (Luke 24:35). In a morning meal of bread and fish, the apostles recognized Jesus on the seashore of Galilee (John 21:12). A little boy brought the small loaves he had and Jesus blessed them, and they were distributed to the 5,000 hungry people on the hillside (John 6:9,11). And on the night of the Last Supper, Jesus takes bread, blesses it, breaks it, and gives it to his friends, saying, "Take and eat"(Matthew 26:26). Finally, in the Our Father, we pray the words "Give us this day our daily bread."

On the Jewish Sabbath, a special braided bread is eaten instead of the bread used for weekday meals. This holiday bread is called *challah* and represents the manna the Israelites received in the desert as described in Exodus 16:22. Challah bread is tithed bread, because a portion is always for the poor. This bread is reminiscent of the Christian Sabbath, when new loaves of bread were served on Sunday morning. In this serving, a cross was made three times on the loaf.

Lammas Day is a time for bread, for kneading it, baking it, breaking it, blessing it, and eating it. It is a time for us to remember that we are called by God to be bread for others. Our hands are God's hands when we make and bake bread, bless and break it with friends, and reach out in our oneness to feed a hungry world. "Because there is one loaf of bread, all of us, though many, are one body, for we all share the same loaf" (1 Corinthians 10:17).

Preparations

directions

Hang the yellow panel for the season of summer.

Before the panel, place a table. On the table place a loaf of bread with a candle in it. Also place a second loaf of bread on the table, for the breaking of the bread. (Since this prayer service lends itself to larger adult and family gatherings, you may want to have small groups, each in a circle around two loaves and a candle.)

During the ceremony, bread will be presented. Have a variety of breads available, either real or shown in pictures.

Choose seven readers.

Choose five people to present "hands."

Place the words "Our hands are God's hands" on the summer panel.

materials

Summer panel
Construction paper
Magic markers
Scissors, pins, tape
Candles
Assortment of breads (or pictures of breads)
Table
Loaf of bread to present

Project

Make a large hand for each of the following: planter, kneader, baker, breaker, and feeder. Place one of these words on each hand.

Divide participants into five groups: planter, kneader, baker, breaker, feeder. Each group writes on one side of their paper hand the ways in which they can serve as that hand for others; for example, ways they can feed others. One member from each group will present the hand and pin it on the panel at an appropriate time during the prayer service.

Make the words "Our hands are God's hands" to be placed on summer panel.

Optional: Make and bake small loaves of bread. Or cut frozen bread from the grocery store into small loaves and bake it.

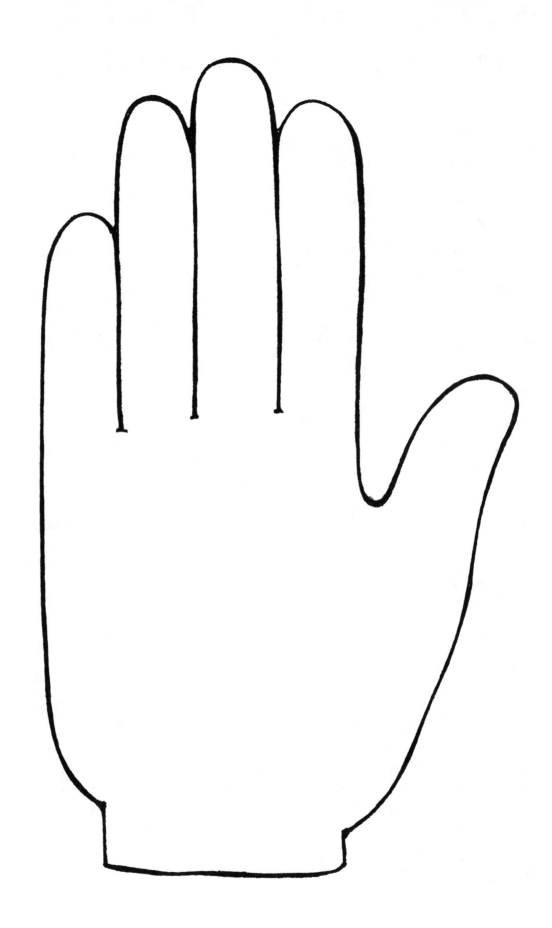

Prayer Celebration

Opening Greeting

LEADER: We gather to celebrate bread in our life. On this day of Lammas, we bless the bread made from the grains of our fields and the work of our hands. Bread speaks of God's presence among and within us. The Lord be with you.

ALL: And also with you.

Bread Presentation

LEADER: Bread is the staff of life. To make bread requires the work of many hands. We open our hands as the hands of the planter.

READER 1: Look at your hands as the hands of the planter. The soil is tilled, and seeds are placed in the earth. Water and sunshine give nourishment as these seeds struggle to grow. As golden fields of wheat, barley, corn, and rye come to harvest, the grain is milled and turned into flour. We say, "Our hands are God's hands when they are the hands of the planter."

ALL: Our hands are God's hands when they are the hands of the planter.

LEADER: We place the hands of the planter on our summer panel.

(pause)

We open our hands as the hands of the kneader.

READER 2: Look at your hands as the hands of the kneader. Yeast is dissolved in water. Then sugar, salt, water, and flour are mixed to become dough. Stiff and heavy the dough is now kneaded. Hands coated with flour flatten the dough, fold it in half, and flatten it again—shaping, changing, molding, and forming the dough. And then hands patiently wait as the dough rises and doubles in size. And then again, shaping, molding, flattening, forming— kneading life. Our hands are God's hands when they are the hands of the kneader.

ALL: Our hands are God's hands when they are the hands of the kneader.

LEADER: We place the hands of the kneader on our summer panel.

(pause)

We open our hands as the hands of the baker.

READER 3: Look at your hands as the hands of the baker. The dough is shaped round, square, oval, or molded into shapes that are signs that express a belief—a heart, a fish, a book, a home. Baking bread warms the hearth, and the smells of fresh baked bread stir the heart and awaken childhood memories. Baked bread delights the eyes and taste in its variety—pumpernickel, Italian, French, Sicilian, Irish soda bread, challah, gingerbread, shortbread, rolls, buns. Our hands are God's hands when they are the hands of the baker.

ALL: Our hands are God's hands when they are the hands of the baker.

LEADER: We place the hands of the baker on our summer panel.

(pause)

We open our hands as the hands that break bread.

READER 4: Look at your hands as the hands that break bread. To break bread is a sign of friendship. Bread fills our hunger for food and for oneness with each other. At breakfast, lunch, supper—at any or all meal times—men, women, and children can be nourished through the bread they eat and through the people who gather to eat. Our hands are God's hands when they are the hands that break bread.

ALL: Our hands are God's hands when they are the hands that break bread.

LEADER: We place the hands that break bread on our summer panel.

(pause and do so)

We open our hands as the hands that feed others.

READER 5: Look at your hands as the hands that feed others. Through large, rough hands, small, slim hands, smooth, round hands, hands that grip tightly and those that touch gently, people are fed. We are brothers and sisters—those who have much and those who have little. We feed others with bread, and we become bread for others. Our hands are God's hands when they are the hands that feed others.

ALL: Our hands are God's hands when they are the hands that feed others.

LEADER: We place the hands that feed others on our summer panel.

(pause)

Lord, God,
You are present in the actions of planting, kneading, baking, breaking, and feeding. Deepen our appreciation of these actions in our life. Give us deep respect for hands, our hands that are yours in our world today. We ask this through your life as creator in each of us.

ALL: Amen.

Blessing of Bread

LEADER: We present and place our breads, the work of many hands, on our table.

(pause and do so)

We extend our hands to bless this bread as we make the sign of the cross three times while praying these words: Bless this bread, Lord.

ALL: Bless this bread, Lord.

(Make the sign of the cross.)

LEADER: May this bread be a sign,

ALL: May this bread be a sign,

(Make the sign of the cross.)

LEADER: of our friendship and oneness.

ALL: of our friendship and oneness.

(Make the sign of the cross.)

LEADER: We open our hands, a sign of our willingness to do your work in the world, Lord.
 (Name of each person) , continue to do the work of God.

(Sign each hand with a cross.)

The Readings

LEADER: To bake bread quickly, yeast as leaven is not used. Because there was not time, unleavened bread was made as the people fled Egypt. Passover celebrates this event. At the friendship meal of the Last Supper, Jesus used unleavened bread.

READER 6: "On the first day of Unleavened Bread, the disciples prepared the Passover meal. As Jesus and his friends sat down at the table, Jesus said, 'I have wanted so much to eat this Passover meal with you.' During this meal, Jesus took bread, blessed it, broke it, and gave it to his friends. 'Take this,' he said, 'This is my body given for you. Take and eat.'"

Luke 22:14, 15, 19 (adapted)

This is the Word of the Lord.

ALL: Thanks be to God.

LEADER: Bread is a sign of unity. Many grains are needed for making the flour and many hands to form the loaf.

READER 7: "The bread we break at the Lord's Supper and for which we give thanks to God; when we eat it, we are sharing in the body of Christ. Because there is the one loaf of bread, we who are many are one body, for we all share the same loaf."

1 Corinthians 10:16–17 (adapted)

This is the Word of the Lord.

ALL: Thanks be to God.

LEADER: As the body of Christ we break and pass this one loaf. As you break a piece, hold it in your hand until all receive.

(pause)

Blessed are you, Lord our God, for giving us this bread to eat.

ALL: Blessed are you, Lord our God, for giving us this bread to eat.

Jesus as the living bread shares his life with us. In our sharing of Jesus' life with each other, we give and receive. Give your piece of bread to the person next to you.

(pause and do so)

Now, take and eat.

Closing Rite of Thanksgiving

LEADER: The whole life of Jesus was an act of loving thanksgiving to God. Let us think for a moment of people, events, and things in our life for which we are thankful.

(pause)

Long ago, it was the custom on the feast of Lammas to place a candle in a loaf of bread and to circle the place of celebration three times. As we pass our Lammas Candle bread, hold it in your hand and offer thanks to God. In turn, pray in your heart a thank you for that person being in our world.

(Pass candle in loaf.)

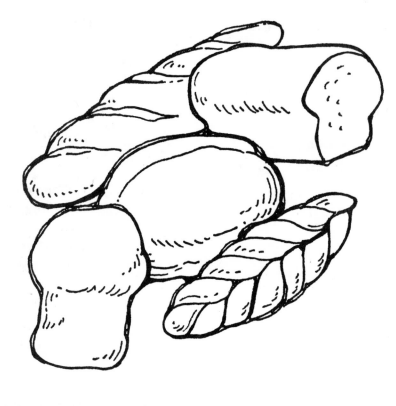

Native Americans' Day

A Background Reflection

Thousands of years before Christopher Columbus reached the western hemisphere, the American Indians made their homes in North and South America. Living simply, they fished and hunted where modern cities now stand, guided canoes quietly along rivers now crowded with ships. With reverence for nature and an intimate relationship with every living creature, they dwelled as community in family and tribe not only with the living but with a deep respect for deceased relatives and friends.

In their celebrations, the Indians emphasized ritual, symbol, and nonverbal communication. The important thing in a ceremony was movement, the dance. Dance conveyed an idea to the spirits and was not performed for the pleasure of an audience. A beating of drums and a shaking of rattles accompanied the movement.

For the Indians, nature was not something outside themselves to be exploited; rather, they felt themselves to be part of nature and honored the gods as found in woods, animals, or the earth. Chief Mountain Lake of the Taos Pueblos said, "We are a people who live on the roof of the world; we are the sons and daughters of Father Sun and with our religion we daily help our father go across the sky. We do this not only for ourselves, but for the whole world. If we were to cease practicing our religion, in ten years the sun would no longer rise. Then it would be night forever." These Indians believed they were partners with God, preserving and sustaining God's gift of creation for all people. We are reminded of Gensis, where God asks that we become stewards and caretakers of the earth.

Because the Indians were so intimately bonded to the land, their ritual ceremonies paralleled their hunting, or their planting and harvesting of the first fruits. Mother Earth, Father Sun, Sister Rain—all were praised and thanked. The seedtime, growth, and harvest of the corn was depicted in a variety of rites and ritual dances. The *kiva*, an underground room for religious ceremonies, welcomed the men of the village. After the ceremony, prayer sticks, lengths of wood with feathers attached, were taken back to their dwellings for continued communication with the spirits. The eternal pattern of seedtime, growth, ripe fruit in the sunshine, rain, and the good harvest was repeated each year.

We are reminded of the scriptural parables of the kingdom shown in the stories of the sower and the farmer and the patterns of seeding, growing, and harvesting. Like the American Indians, we know that though we sow and reap, it is still God who has made the seed grow and has brought it to harvest.

There were many, diverse Indian tribes. Some lived by hunting and gathering nuts, seeds, and roots; others planted gardens. Some made their dwellings in teepees, other in adobe homes. In North America alone, there was once over 300 tribal languages and countless dialects.

By the time the white settlers came to America, our native Americans had explored almost all the land, discovered important natural resources, found the easiest trails over mountains and across rivers. As newcomers, the settlers were guided by the Indians to mineral springs and mineral deposits, shown how to travel by canoe and snowshoes, and taught how to grow food. Having developed wild plants into useful food through thousands of years of cultivation, the settlers were shown how to cook the food. And throughout the bitter cold winters of the settlers' early years when food was scarce, the Indians were generous in offering their own food.

As settlers went westward, the Indians were forced farther away from their homelands. When they stopped to defend themselves, they were forcibly overwhelmed by the whites. Banding together under leaders like King Philip, Pontiac, and Tecumseh, they were overcome again not only by their opponents but in the realization of how different they were as individual tribes. The defeated Indians were placed on reservation lands that had little or no value.

In 1915, at the annual assembly of the American Indian Association, over a thousand Indians representing more than a hundred tribes voted approval of an annual American Indian Day. Sherman Coolidge, an Arapahoe Indian and president of the assembly, urged recognition of Indian citizenship and Indian loyalty: "We declare our needs now and tomorrow as those primarily of Americans struggling for enlightenment and competency that are consistent with American citizenship. May this day be observed as a memorial to the Indian race and to a wise consideration of its future as part of the American people." Today, most states celebrate Native American Day on the fourth Friday in September. Some states observe this day on the second Saturday in May or select a day during the year convenient for all residents.

The Indians' road to citizenship in a country where they had lived all their lives was slow and arduous. Only in 1924 was citizenship granted to all Indians born in the United States, and only by 1948 were American Indians finally able to vote in all states.

Throughout our country, we have reminders of America's roots in an Indian culture— thousands of Indian names of rivers, towns, cities, and states, as well as the words and concepts that are now part of our everyday speech, such as *toboggan, tobacco, moccasin,* and *raccoon.* Indian foods are still eaten today: succotash, hominy, squash. Today many societies and museums throughout the country, such as the Institute of American Indian Art in New Mexico, the Museum of the American Indian in New York, offer in their collections the richness and variety of Indian culture and their contribution to the formation of our own culture.

Preparations

directions

Hang the orange panel for the season of fall.

Choose six readers. Choose a narrator or let the leader do this part also.

Place four candles to form a circle (or, if you have a Yule Wheel, use it). Indicate north, south, east, and west for each candle. Place the Wheel before the panel.

Choose people to use prayer sticks and other sounds.

Choose people to present the sun, green shoots, blades, grain ears, ripe grain.

Show all participants the movement for each part of the parable of the farmer. This movement is to give them an experience of a ritual pattern as expressed by American Indians in dance.

materials

Orange panel
Yule Wheel
Candles
Prayer sticks
Sound makers
Construction paper
Magic markers
Scissors
Ribbons, feathers
Pins or tape

Project

Make a sign for each of earth's directions: north, south, east, west.

Make a sun, green shoots, blades, green ears of grain, ripe grain.

Make prayer sticks (use branches found outdoors). Put ribbons, feathers, and strips of paper on them.

Prayer Celebration

Opening Greeting

LEADER: We gather to give thanks and recognition to our native Americans. We thank God for their presence on our planet Earth and for showing us how to respect all of life. The Spirit of God be with you.

ALL: And also with you.

LEADER: Let us listen to the plea of an Arapahoe Indian for a day of recognition for our native Americans.

READER 1: "We do invite all Americans who love their country and would uphold its honor and dignity, to celebrate this day and to consider our early philosophy, our love of freedom, our social institutions, and our history in the full light of truth and the balance of justice, in honest comparison with the annals of other races and to draw therefrom these noble things that we believe are worthy of emulation. We call upon our country to consider the past, but to earnestly consider our present and our future as a part of the American people. To them we declare our needs now and tomorrow as those primarily of Americans struggling for enlightment."
Sherman Coolidge, an Arapahoe

Proclamation at the Assembly of the American Indian Association 1915

LEADER: The wheel stands as a way of life. Within its circle one sees all people as a whole.

READER 2: At the place of north we light this candle in thanksgiving for the Chippewa, Sioux, Cree, Cheyenne, Winnebago, Ottawa, Crow, Blackfoot, Chinook, Shoshoni, Comanche, Dakota.

(pause and do so)

READER 3: At the place of west, we light this candle in thanksgiving for the Arapahoe, Pueblo, Apache, Navaho, Hopi, Ute, Maidu, Pomo, Yuma, Mohave.

(pause)

READER 4: At the place of south, we light this candle in thanksgiving for the Seminole, Cherokee, Shawnee, Chickasaw, Creek, Chocktaw, Natchez, Quapaw, Tuscarora.

(pause)

READER 5: At the place of east, we light this candle in thanksgiving for the Delaware, Mohegan, Iroquois, Mohawk, Cayuga, Oneida, Seneca, Narraganset, Algonquin, Massachuset.

(pause)

The One Journey

LEADER: We are one people. Like our native Americans, we invite and welcome the ancients, our invisible companions, as guests in our daily living. We remember all people who have walked this earth from the beginning of time

(pause—sound of prayer sticks)

and we welcome them as guests for our journey of life. We remember all family members who have died, those most recent and those of long ago

(pause—sound of prayer sticks)

and we welcome them as guests for our journey of life. We remember Jesus and the promise of his spirit with us always.

(pause—sound of prayer sticks)

and we welcome this spirit as guest for our journey of life. Lord, our God, God of our mothers and fathers, God of Abraham and Sarah, God of Isaac and Rebecca, God of Jacob and Rachel, be present with us now as we gently walk your earth and touch with reverence your creation. We welcome you, and all people that you have made into our hearts. May we be guests to one another. We ask this of you as creator and sustainer of all life.

(pause—sound of prayer sticks)

ALL: Amen.

Rite of Growing

LEADER: Scripture teaches us about the Kingdom of God in the pattern of seeding, growing, and harvesting. We learn from our native Americans a respect and reverence for this pattern expressed in their dance rituals.

NARRATOR: One day the sun was shining brightly.

(gesture, sound—sun is placed on panel)

And a farmer went out and scattered seed on the ground.

(gesture, sound—seed placed on panel)

The farmer prays for rain.

(gesture, sound)

The farmer goes to bed and sleeps.

(gesture, sound)

The farmer awakens at day

(gesture, sound)

and sleeps at night.

(gesture, sound)

And through all those nights and days, the seed begins to sprout of their own accord. First, the shoot,

(gesture, sound—shoot placed on panel)

then the blades,

(gesture, sound—blade placed on panel)

then the ear,

(gesture, sound—ear placed on panel)

and then the full grain in the ear.

(gesture, sound—grain placed on panel)

And when the crop is ready, the farmer begins to reap for the time of harvest has come.

(gesture, sound)

Based on Mark 4:26-29

LEADER: **We remember from this story that though we may sow the seed and reap, still it is God who has made the seed to grow and has brought it to the harvest. It takes time and patience for the Kingdom of God to grow. In our journey together, we, too, are seeds, we are the kingdom that is daily growing.**

Lord,
Give us sun to warm our hearts and rain to nourish our spirits so we may growing in your likeness. Our response will be, "Lord, we are the work of your hands. Let us know that wherever we are in our growing, it is a good and holy place to be.
Lord, we are the work of your hands."

ALL: **Lord, we are the work of your hands.**

LEADER: **Give us honest acceptance of who we are and who others are in relation to us.**
"Lord, we are the work of your hands."

ALL: **Lord, we are the work of your hands.**

LEADER: **Give us sleep at night and wakefulness during the day as we live your life for others.**
"Lord, we are the work of your hands."

ALL: **Lord, we are the work of your hands.**

LEADER: **Let us know the time of planting, of reaping, and of harvesting and give us patience to see the time as your time.**
"Lord, we are the work of your hands."

ALL: **Lord, we are the work of your hands.**

Closing Blessing

LEADER: Let us sit. Become quiet inside. We are the inner circle of the wheel, we are one, we are the people of God. As God's people, let us close our eyes and listen to the Spirit through the words of the Plains Indians.

READER 6: "Come sit with me and let us smoke the Pipe of Peace in Understanding. Let us touch. Let us, each to the other, be a Gift as is the Buffalo. Let us be Meat to Nourish each other, that we may all Grow. Sit here with me, each of you as you are in your own Perceiving of yourself. Let me see through your Eyes. Let us teach each other here in this great Lodge of the people, this Sun Dance, of each of the Ways on this Great Medicine Wheel, our earth."

Seven Arrows, Hyemeyohsts Storm

LEADER: Lift your hands, hearts, and heads for God's blessing. May we be gift.

ALL: Amen.

LEADER: May we nourish each other for growth.

ALL: Amen.

LEADER: May we learn the ways of God's earth.

ALL: Amen.

LEADER: We go forth in peace. In our homes we place our prayer sticks. May they daily remind us of God's spirit in all the moments of our daily living and growing. In the name of God the Creator, the Son the Redeemer, and the Spirit the Giver of Life.

ALL: Amen.

Harvest Day

A Background Reflection

Since people first planted grain in the earth and watched it grow and ripen, there have been harvest festivals. We all seem to have a universal need to give thanks to our God for the fruits of the earth.

In Greece these festivals gave tribute to the grain goddess Demeter. Other countries addressed this goddess as "Mother of Grains," or "Mother of Fields." Ancient belief in this great Mother can be seen even today with the superstition accorded the last sheaf in every field. In France, the last sheaf is tied in the form of a cross, decorated with ribbons and flowers, and displayed in the home as a sign of blessing. In England we find the last sheaf being braided into a doll, dressed with flowers and ribbons, and displayed on a pole for all to see, or ceremoniously thrown into the river to ensure plenty of rain for next year's crops. In Austria, the last sheaf was shaped into a wreath and placed as a crown on the village girl designated as Harvest Queen. In Poland, the harvest wreaths decorated with flowers, apples, nuts, and ribbons are reminiscent of the one we see on doors or in people's homes today.

Our earliest roots in giving thanks come from Moses, instituting two great thanksgiving feasts among the Hebrews: Feast of Spring Harvest, Shavout, and the Feast of Fall Harvest, Sukkot. Sukkot represents the fresh start of a new year and the same time the harvest of the old year. It is a holiday to celebrate all growing plants. During this weeklong festival, a booth or hut, a *sukkah* was built. The Book of Leviticus describes the manner in which a *sukkah* was constructed: three walls, a branch-covered roof with an opening to the sky. This opening allowed the stars to be seen and rain to be received, both reminding the people of God beyond. The *sukkah* is decorated with fruits and vegetables.

This dwelling in booths probably originated as a temporary dwelling for harvesters to finish work in the field without having to journey home; they are also symbolic of the makeshift dwellings the people made as they wandered in the desert for forty years. These booths remind us of a simpler life, closer to nature. As symbols, they suggest that life, though precarious and transient, is still filled with richness, color, and joy. The tabernacle in Christian churches, is a direct descendant of the tabernacle, tent, or *sukkah* that was the first holy dwelling in the wilderness.

New England pilgrims who commemorated their harvest with a feast of Thanksgiving probably used Sukkot as a model. For these pilgrims, who had survived their first bitter winter, their first harvest was a time for rejoicing. The Indians had shared their seeds of corn (maize). When the corn was harvested, there was celebration and thanksgiving. For the Indians gathered at this Thanksgiving feast, it was a reminder of their own harvest celebration for the previous hundreds of years. This Pilgrim Thanksgiving and the foods served then became the pattern for our present Thanksgiving—turkey, apple cider, pumpkin pie, nuts, and an abundance of all the fruits of autumn. In all fifty states, Thanksgiving is now celebrated on the fourth Thursday in November; in Canada, on the second Monday in October.

The autumnal equinox that marks the official change of season is situated halfway between the summer and winter solstice. On this day the sun crosses the equator from north to south. For the Northern Hemisphere, this date is usually September 23. On this day, as with the vernal equinox of March 21, day and night are of equal length. So we have three things in common with our brothers and sisters around the planet Earth at this time of the year—the experience of equal day and night, the wonder in our hearts as we gather to partake of the abundance produced by the good earth at harvest, and the call to share that plenty with those in need.

The season of autumn has always played a vivid role in the life of the farmer. Autumn remains the period of harvest, vintage, and fruit gathering. The harvest moon—the full moon nearest the time of the equinox—appears above the horizon at about sunset for a number of days and provides light for farmers to harvest into the night. Americans call this season fall, which means the time when the red and golden leaves fall from trees. Autumn can be sad, because summer and outdoor living is over, but it is also a happy time, because it is the season of harvest. Many people of the world, whose calendars differ from ours, now celebrate their New Year. For them the autumn also reflects the two moods, joy for a new year's beginning and sadness for the old year's end. But, always, permeating both moods, is the need to say thanks for all gifts great and small.

Preparations

directions

Hang the orange panel for the autumn season horizontally—this will suggest the *sukkah*.

Define the space of your *sukkah* before the orange panel. Explain what a *sukkah* is and how and why it was constructed.

Alert the participants that they will be called by name during the prayer service to gather and sit in this *sukkah*.

Choose one reader.

Choose four people to present the autumn fruits, seeds, bread, and juice that will be placed in the center of the gathering.

materials

Fruits, seeds, bread, juice
Decorations for the *sukkah*—branches, leaves, vegetables, streamers, etc.

Project

Make a *sukkah* (tentlike dwelling). Be as elaborate as you wish or simply use the orange panel draped horizontally. Decorate with fall leaves, corn husks, wheat sheafs, grapes, autumn vegetables, and fruits.

Prayer Celebration

Opening Greeting

LEADER: Autumn is the season of gathering, a time of harvest. In thanksgiving, we bow our heads in gratitude for all God's blessings. In praise we rejoice in the goodness of life. The Lord be with you.

ALL: And also with you.

LEADER: Lift up your hearts.

ALL: We lift them up to the Lord.

LEADER: Let us give thanks to the Lord our God.

ALL: It is right to give God thanks and praise.

The Gathering Call

LEADER: At the time of the autumnal equinox, the position of the sun offers to every place on earth, equal length of day and night. To all places, east and west, north and south, the call goes out to gather together the harvest of the earth and the people of the harvest:
Come, _____(Names)_____ welcome to the dwelling place of the Lord.

(Call participants in groups of four to take their place in the sukkah.)

And to this dwelling place of the Lord we bring the harvest of the earth. We bring the autumn fruits and say, "Thank you, Lord, for the harvest of your earth."

ALL: Thank you, Lord, for the harvest of your earth.

LEADER: We bring autumn seeds and say, "Thank you, Lord, for the harvest of your earth."

ALL: Thank you, Lord, for the harvest of your earth.

LEADER: We bring sheafs of autumn grains made into bread, and say, "Thank you, Lord, for the harvest of your earth."

ALL: Thank you, Lord, for the harvest of your earth.

LEADER: We bring autumn grapes made into wine, and say, "Thank you, Lord, for the harvest of your earth."

ALL: Thank you, Lord, for the harvest of your earth.

The Gathered

LEADER: And we ask, why do we gather together? Why do we come to this pilgrim feast of the Lord? Why do we give thanks? And for our answers we listen with our hearts to God's word to us in scripture.

READER 1: "The Lord said to Moses. Speak to the Israelites and tell them: There are many festivals of the Lord, my feast days, which I ask you to celebrate with a sacred assembly. At one of these, the Feast of Booths, I ask you to gather the produce of the land and celebrate for a week a pilgrim feast of the Lord. On the first day gather branches of palms, myrtles, and poplars and make merry before the Lord your God. During this week, I ask you to dwell in booths, that your descendants may realize that when I led the Israelites out of the land of Egypt, I made them dwell in booths. I, the Lord, am your God."

Leviticus 23:1, 2, 34, 39–43 (adapted)

This is the Word of the Lord.

ALL: Thanks be to God.

LEADER: We are a sacred people for the Lord dwells among us and within us. In this gathering place, we celebrate as a sacred assembly. Here in our booth we make merry before the Lord. Through our opening to the sky, we welcome sun, moon, stars, all God's gifts, and we say,

ALL: It is right to give God thanks and praise.

Psalm 92:2

LEADER: With tree branches, fruits, and vegetables of the harvest, all God's gifts, we say,

ALL: It is right to give God thanks and praise.

LEADER: With colored leaves, signs of the changing season, all God's gifts, we say,

ALL: It is right to give God thanks and praise.

LEADER: With sheafs and bread, grapes and wine, all God's gifts, we say,

ALL: It is right to give God thanks and praise.

LEADER: From our Hebrew traditions and heritage, we now bless these gifts:

(Take bread and hold it.)

Blessed are you, Lord our God, king of the universe,

ALL: Blessed are you, Lord our God, king of the universe,

LEADER: who gives to us bread,

ALL: who gives to us bread,

LEADER: and causes the earth to overflow with good for all.

ALL: and causes the earth to overflow with good for all.

(Pass bread; take the wine [juice] and hold it.)

LEADER: Blessed are you, Lord our God, king of the universe,

ALL: Blessed are you, Lord our God, king of the universe,

LEADER: who from the vine has created the gift of wine,

ALL: who from the vine has created the gift of wine,

LEADER: a sign of our love and unity.

ALL: a sign of our love and unity.

(Pass wine; take the seeds and hold them.)

LEADER: Blessed are you, Lord our God, king of the universe,

ALL: Blessed are you, Lord our God, king of the universe,

LEADER: who gives us seedtime and harvest,

ALL: who gives us seedtime and harvest,

LEADER: a sign of your faithful presence within us and all creation.

ALL: a sign of your faithful presence within us and all creation.

(Pass seeds.)

LEADER: Lord,
You are our God, our creator. You sustain us with your life. Give us hearts that rejoice in the wondrous gifts of the earth. Give us hands that share these gifts with all those in need wherever they may be. This harvest reveals your goodness, Lord. As people of the harvest, continue to gather us and all creation into your shelter of peace where we will dwell with you forever.

ALL: Amen.

Closing Blessing

LEADER: As a gesture of thanks, we stand, raise our heads, and open our hands in gratitude to the Lord, our God.
The earth has yielded its fruits; God our God has blessed us.

Psalm 67:7

ALL: Amen.

LEADER: God made the moon to mark the seasons and
the sun to know the hour of its setting.

Psalm 104:19

ALL: Amen.

LEADER: Many will gather from the east and west and will find a place in the banquet in the kingdom of God.

Matthew 8:11

ALL: Amen.

LEADER: Let us go forth as God's gathering people and share the richness of the harvest with all God's creation.

ALL: So be it. So be it. So be it.

LEADER: To our home meals we now bring our loaves of bread. Share them with your family and symbolically with all God's people. With the crumbs, feed the birds, as a sign that our hands care for all God's creation.

ALL: Together we ask God to daily give us bread to eat through the prayer Jesus taught us:
OUR FATHER, WHO ART IN HEAVEN, HALLOWED BE YOUR NAME, YOUR KINGDOM COME, YOUR WILL BE DONE ON EARTH AS IT IS IN HEAVEN. GIVE US THIS DAY OUR DAILY BREAD AND FORGIVE US OUR TRESPASSES AS WE FORGIVE THOSE WHO TRESPASS AGAINST US. AND LEAD US NOT INTO TEMPTATION BUT DELIVER US FROM EVIL. FOR YOURS IS THE KINGDOM AND THE GLORY NOW AND FOREVER. AMEN.

Columbus Day

A Background Reflection

"Land! Land!" After thirty-three days of crossing unknown seas, these words brought rejoicing to the crew and captain of the three small Spanish ships, the *Nina*, the *Pinta*, and the *Santa Maria*. On reaching shore, Christopher Columbus knelt and thanked God for a safe voyage. From Columbus's journal, we read this entry: "Friday, 12th of October. . . . The admiral took and planted on the earth the royal standard with two other banners of the green cross. These two banners had an *F* and a *Y* (Fernando and Ysabel) and a crown over each letter, one on one side of the cross, and the other on the other side. We saw trees very green, and much water, and fruits of diverse kinds."

Columbus felt that divine guidance was with him in all his explorations. His faith gave him the courage to enter unknown territory. Confident in his belief that Earth was round, Columbus was determined to find a short route to India. Since he miscalculated Earth's size and did not realize that the ocean surrounding Japan was not the same as the one along the shores of Spain, he persisted in his belief that he had reached the Indies and returned in triumph to Spain and to his benefactors.

Born in Genoa, Italy, Columbus was a self-taught man, persuasive in his beliefs; a capable sea commander; and a careful and accurate navigator. He discovered the best way to use winds for transatlantic sailing, began the European settlement of the West Indies, and made the first European exploration of South America and the western Caribbean. He made four voyages in all to this "new world" but he found none of the spices and wealth of the Indies for which he was searching.

An Italian, Americus Vespucius, who explored the coast of South America after Columbus, told thrilling stories of his voyages. As these stories circulated, a German map maker identified the new land on his map by printing the word "America" across it.

Columbus reminds us of the courage it takes to travel new roads and the confidence that is needed to begin our travel. We are reminded of the call of God to Abraham and Sarah to leave their homeland and travel to a new land. That same call comes to each of us. It is a call not only to travel in the space we know but to take the unknown inner journey to discover who we each are as persons and who together we might be as a people. Let us make our land a home where freedom, peace, and justice are for all people. In the words of the poet Lord Tennyson, "Let us seek and strive for a better world."

Preparations

directions

Hang the orange panel for season of spring.

Choose three readers.

Place a candle in front of the panel.

On the orange panel, display the flag Columbus planted in America.

Display a map of America.

Have family signs ready for participants to place on American map.

materials

Orange panel
American map
Construction paper
Magic markers
Scissors
Pins or tape
Candle

Project

On the orange panel, make a cross with a crown in each of the top portions of the letters *F* and *Y* in each of the lower portions.

Outline a map of America.

Each participant chooses and makes a family sign. He or she will place these signs on the map for places where the family has lived or traveled.

Prayer Celebration

Opening Greeting

LEADER: This is the land of America. Long ago, one man, Christopher Columbus, reached far beyond the world he lived in. With courage and confidence, he sailed in search of a new land, a land that became a home for people of all nations who would one day also leave their homelands. How does one trust the vision? Where does one find the courage? How does one reach beyond the known? We listen to the poet for the faith that is needed to light unknown paths.

READER 1: "O, World, thou choosest not the better part.
It is not wisdom to be only wise,
And on the inward vision close the eye.
But it is wisdom to believe the heart.
Columbus found a world, and had no chart,
Save one that faith deciphered in the skies;
To trust the soul's invincible surmise
Was all his science and his only art.
Our knowledge is a torch of smoky pine
That lights the pathway but one step ahead
Across a void of mystery and dread.
Bid the tender light of faith to shine
By which alone the moral heart is led
Unto the thinking of the thought divine.

O World, George Santayana

Our Traveled Land

LEADER: We have placed the map of America by the flag Christopher Columbus planted in the earth of this land. We light this candle. It is with the light of faith that we venture forth across our land.

(pause)

As your name is called, come forward and place on our map your family sign for places you have traveled. Mark those places where relatives and friends now live.

(pause)

Let us listen to God's words of sending to a new land.

READER 2: "Go forth from the land of your kinsfolk and from your father's house to a land that I will show you. Abraham was seventy-five years old when he left his homeland. Abraham took his wife Sarah, his brother's son, Lot, all the possessions that they had accumulated and acquired and set out to the land of Canaan. When they arrived, Abraham pitched his tent and built an altar to the Lord and called the Lord by name."

Genesis 12:1, 4, 5, 7

This is the Word of the Lord.

ALL: Thanks be to God.

LEADER: Like Abraham, Christopher Columbus, on reaching land, knelt down and gave thanks to God for a safe voyage. For these people and their journeys, we, too, thank God: For Noah, his wife and family on the ark, for Abraham and Sarah leaving their homeland, for Moses and Miriam leading the people across the desert, like them, We call you by name, Lord, you are our God.

ALL: We call you by name, Lord, you are our God.

LEADER: For Isaiah, Jeremiah, Amos, and Jonah, prophets who traveled to towns, villages, cities, and countries, like them, We call you by name, Lord, you are our God.

ALL: We call you by name, Lord, you are our God.

LEADER: For fishermen Peter and Andrew, James and John, for disciples Paul, Timothy, Barnabas, Luke, for truth seekers Mary, Elizabeth, Magdalene, Martha, Anna, like them, We call you by name, Lord, you are our God.

ALL: We call you by name, Lord, you are our God.

LEADER: For explorers and missionaries, navigators and astronauts, for those journeying through outer space and the inner space of the heart, like them, We call you by name, Lord, you are our God.

ALL: We call you by name, Lord, you are our God.

LEADER: For our mothers, fathers, sisters, brothers, relatives, and friends, for each of us who have the courage to seek and reach beyond to mystery, like them, We call you by name, Lord, you are our God.

ALL: We call you by name, Lord, you are our God.

LEADER: Lord,
Give us light, your light for our journey. Instill in our hearts a deep faith in your presence in us and in our world. Protect and guide us on all paths we travel. We ask this in your name, Lord, our God.

ALL: Amen.

Rite of Journey

LEADER: We are all travelers on our planet Earth. God calls us and we respond. Whatever our choice, the traveled or untraveled path, we know God walks with us.

READER 3: Two roads diverged in a yellow wood, and sorry I
could not travel both and be one traveler,
Long I stood and looked down one as far as I could
to where it bent in the undergrowth;
Then took the other, as just as fair,
And having perhaps the better claim,
Because it was grassy and wanted wear;
Though as for that the pass there had worn them
really about the same,
And both that morning equally lay
In leaves no step had trodden black.
Oh, I kept the first for another day.
Yet knowing how way leads on to way,
I doubted if I should ever come back.
I shall be telling this with a sign
Somewhere ages and ages hence;
Two roads diverged in a wood, and I—
I took the one less traveled by,
And that had made all the difference.

Robert Frost, *The Road Not Taken*

LEADER: As a traveler on this planet earth, are you more likely to choose a worn and traveled path, or make your own path as you go?

(pause)

Think of the last time you had to make a choice in your direction in life? Was it easy? Hard?

(pause)

What path has made all the difference in your own life?

(pause)

In all our roads of life, let us praise the Lord.
Let us sing for joy to God who protects us.
Let us come before God with thanksgiving and make
a joyful noise with songs of praise.
Come, let us praise the Lord.

ALL: Come, let us praise the Lord.

LEADER: For the Lord is a great God, a mighty king
who rules over all the earth from the deepest
caves to the highest hills.
Come, let us praise the Lord.

ALL: Come, let us praise the Lord.

LEADER: God rules over the sea; God's hands farmed the dry land,
Come, let us worship and bow down before God
our maker. We are the people for whom God provides
and protects; we are the sheep of God's hand.
Come, let us praise the Lord.

ALL: Come, let us praise the Lord.

Psalm 95:1–5 (adapted)

Closing Blessing: Blessing for Travel

LEADER: God calls us to travel the known and unknown paths of life. With all explorers and navigators, missionaries, and seekers, we bow our head for God's blessing of light and faith. Lord, protect the way.

ALL: Protect the way.

LEADER: Lighten our traveling feet.

ALL: Lighten our traveling feet.

LEADER: Guide and direct our restless spirits.

ALL: Guide and direct our restless spirits.

LEADER: Answer the needs of our searching hearts.

ALL: Answer the needs of our searching hearts.

LEADER: Make safe all the roads of life.

ALL: Make safe all the roads of life.

LEADER: And make our journey, your journey, Lord.

ALL: And make our journey, your journey, Lord.

LEADER: And now as you go on your way:
May the road rise up to meet you.
May the wind be always at your back.
May the sun shine warm upon your face, the rains fall soft upon your fields.
And, until we meet again,
May you be held in the palm of God's hand.

An Irish Blessing

ALL: Amen.

Halloween

A Background Reflection

In the eighth century A.D., Gregory III had established the festival of All Saints Day (All Hallows) on November 1. In the next century, Gregory IV decreed the day to be a universal church observance in honor of all saints who died with or without church recognition of sanctity. On the next day (November 2), All Souls' Day, prayers are offered for the dead.

Medieval celebrations of New Year, May Day, Midsummer, and All Hallows shared similar festival activities. Centered around fire, the great medieval halls were decorated, mummers (bands of masked persons who danced in silence) performed, elaborate food was served, and games played. Presiding over the festivities were usually a king or queen for the evening. On All Hallows, someone dressed as King Crispin in regal robes with a large medallion on which was designed one big foot. This king—really St. Crispin—is the patron saint of shoemakers and cobblers. It is said that he preached all day and then worked with his hands all night, making shoes and giving praise to God in the very work he did.

These medieval Halloween festivals combined pagan customs of summer's end with Christian ones. Children wearing masks would go "souling" from door to door, singing and begging for soul cakes (flat, oval shortbread cookies with currants, cinnamon, and nutmeg) for wandering spirits. If no treats were offered, pranks were played.

Fire, a symbol of immortality among the ancients, was used on this night to welcome good spirits and prevent evil ones from coming near. Hollowed-out turnips, squash, or rutabagas were fashioned, with cut-out faces of grins or scowls. A lighted candle was placed inside. These were called Jack O'Lanterns. Irish legend says that a man named Jack was kept out of heaven because of his stinginess but not allowed to enter hell because of the jokes he played on the devil. So now he must roam the earth carrying a lantern. Pumpkins were first used after the discovery of America.

Children carried these jack o'lanterns to protect themselves from evil spirits and welcome good ones. Many farmers carried torches around the perimeter of fields, to scare away demons and protect crops while offering light to welcome the good spirits.

During October, supernatural beings were thought to be most powerful and lonely. They roamed the land as ghosts, fairies, elves, goblins, leprechauns, witches, and all kinds of supernatural beings. It became the custom of the day of Halloween to ask these spirits questions about love, life, and the identity of one's future spouse.

Apples were both used for fortune telling and for games. If you took an apple and pared it in one continuous length, twirled it around your head three times, and let it fall over your left shoulder, you would discover in the shape it took, the initials of your lover. Ducking for apples and biting at apples suspended from a string remain popular in America today.

Halloween in America today remains a favorite day for children but a worrisome one for parents. Communities have become concerned. With proper chaperoning and guidance, this holiday could offer an experience of treating property and people with respect as well as receiving treats from others. Many children carry UNICEF boxes and collect money for poor children of the world. This money goes to the United Nations fund and becomes a way of offering what we have to our less fortunate brothers and sisters around the world. In this way, we, indeed, become wandering spirits for others.

Preparations

directions

Hang the orange panel for the season of fall. Place a table before the panel and on it put smiling and frowning jack o'lanterns.

Choose three participants to place the three baskets on this table during prayer service.

Participants should have their jack o'lantern faces with them.

Choose tambourine players.

Choose someone to play King Crispin, and costume that person.

Have shoes for presenting.

Be prepared to call participants by name.

Choose two readers.

Three baskets should be filled with apples, nuts, and soul cakes.

materials

Construction paper
Scissors
Magic markers
Tambourines
Baskets
Apples, nuts, soul cakes
Table
Orange panel

Project

Make two one-dimensional jack o'lantern faces —one smiling, the other frowning. Cut out nose, eyes, mouth. Place a candle behind each. Or carve out two real pumpkins. Place a candle inside each.

Have each participant make a jack o'lantern face—either a smiling or a frowning one. Cut out.

Dress King Crispin in a robe. Make a large medallion with a shoe on it.

Make or buy small cakes (shortbread cookies).

Make a "shoe" for each participant of construction paper.

Prayer Celebration

Opening Greeting

LEADER: We gather together to celebrate the spirit of God alive within each of us. In this Spirit, we ask guidance and protection for all the days and nights of our life.

Light of Jack O'Lanterns

LEADER: This is the eve for merrymaking, the eve for lighting fire to welcome good spirits and to prevent not-so-good spirits from coming near. We light the candle of our smiling jack o'lantern and we say, "Lord, we are thankful." For the times we choose to walk happily and friendly in your light,

ALL: Lord, we are thankful.

LEADER: For the times we are able to see your light in the people we meet,

ALL: Lord, we are thankful.

LEADER: For the times we recognize your smiling light living deep in our heart,

ALL: Lord, we are thankful.

LEADER: We light the candle of our frowning jack o'lantern and we say, "Lord, we are sorry." For the times we walked with grumpy and frowning faces thinking only of ourselves,

ALL: Lord, we are sorry.

LEADER: For the times we closed our eyes to the needs of others,

ALL: Lord, we are sorry.

LEADER: For the times we did not live in your light,

ALL: Lord, we are sorry.

LEADER: We hold up our own jack o'lantern face. Through its smiles or frowns, the light of your spirit in us, Lord, continues to shine through for everyone to see.

(Everyone holds up jack o'lantern face.)

Lord,
we thank you for the light of your spirit, which continues to shine through all times so that together we bless ourselves in your presence.

ALL: In the name of the Father, and of the Son, and of the Holy Spirit. Amen.

The Journey Presentation

LEADER: To our celebration we welcome King Crispin, patron of shoemakers and all people who help our feet walk the height and depth, width and breadth of this earth.

(King Crispin arrives. Tambourines play.)

On our feast table, we place three baskets of food—
a basket of apples—

(Tambourines play.)

a basket of nuts—

(tambourines)

and a basket of soul cakes.

(tambourines)

Life is a journey. Where we are going and how we will get there are questions that life daily offers us. On this journey we know that we have God's protection and we need never walk alone. Let us listen to this scripture story, which tells of God's promise of protection as we walk this earth.

READER 1: **"Jacob left Beersheba and started toward Haran. At sunset he came to a holy place and camped there. He lay down to sleep, resting his head on a stone. He dreamed that he saw a stairway reaching from earth to heaven, with angels going up and coming down on it. And there was the Lord standing beside him. 'I am the Lord, the God of Abraham and Isaac,' he said. 'I will give to you and to your descendants this land on which you are living. They will be as numerous as the specks of dust on the earth. They will extend their territory in all directions, and through you and your descendants, I will bless all nations. Remember, I will be with you and protect you wherever you go, and I will bring you back to this land."**

Genesis 28:10–15 GNB

This is the Word of the Lord.

ALL: **Thanks be to God.**

LEADER: **As your name is called, come forward and receive a sign of your willingness to walk this earth under God's protection. _____(Name)_____, know that God is with you.**

(Pin paper shoe on each participant.)

Trick or Treat

LEADER: **On Halloween night, we are all trick or treaters. Like the soulers of old, we wear our masks and ask for treats for our wandering spirits. We extend one hand before us as we circle the room.**

(Tambourines play during chant.)

Souling, souling, for soul cakes we go,

ALL: **Souling, souling, for soul cakes we go.**

LEADER: **One for Peter, two for Paul,**

ALL: **One for Peter, two for Paul.**

LEADER: **Three for him who made us all.**

ALL: **Three for him who made us all.**

LEADER: **If you haven't got a cake, an apple will do,**

ALL: **If you haven't got a cake, an apple will do.**

LEADER: **If you haven't got an apple, give a nut or two.**

ALL: **If you haven't got an apple, give a nut or two.**

LEADER: If you haven't got a nut, then God bless you.

ALL: If you haven't got a nut, then God bless you.

(Chant and circle twice, wearing masks. As the chanters pass the head table during the second round, they are invited to take from the apple, nut, or soul cake baskets.)

We need never play tricks on others, for God is generous through the people who love and care for us.

A Closing Blessing: Blessing Before Travel on Halloween Night

LEADER: Let us listen to these words of scripture.

READER 2: "Before setting out on his journey, the young Tobiah kissed his father and mother. His father Tobit said to him, 'Have a safe journey' and spoke comforting words to the worried mother— 'Our child leaves in good health and will come back to us in good health. Your own eyes will see his safe return. So, do not worry, my love. For a good spirit will go with him and he will return unharmed.'"

Tobit 5:17–22 (adapted)

This is the Word of the Lord.

ALL: Thanks be to God.

LEADER: We ask God's blessing for each of us as we travel. Our response will be, "Lord, be with us." That you may safely walk the streets of your neighborhood,

ALL: Lord, be with us.

LEADER: That you may treat others kindly and not trick them by what you do or say,

ALL: Lord, be with us.

LEADER: That the Spirit protect and guide you and return you home in peace and joy.

ALL: Lord, be with us.

LEADER: Lord, God,
Guide our friends as they begin their journey. Bless them with peace as they travel and bring them home safely. Let us go forth in the peace and love of Christ and become his wandering spirits on this eve of All Hallows.

ALL: Amen.

World Peace Day

A Background Reflection

The vision of peace begins and develops through God's relationship with people. Founded on justice, peace is a result of God's loving and forgiving presence among us: "I am your God. You are my people. I love you. Love me. Love one another. Be my friend. Be the friend of others." Through the Hebrew scriptures, we understand this promise of love and friendship, and we discover that peace comes through fidelity to the covenant relationship.

In the Christian scriptures, we discover Jesus as God's peace. Through Jesus we continue to be formed and shaped as friends of God and one another. In his active love for all people, Jesus is the model of peacemaking and challenges us to become ministers of reconciliation as we allow God to change us from enemies into friends and become one with God and one with all that God has made.

On the last weekend in May 1983, over 10,000 Catholics, Protestants, and Jewish congregations in the United States participated in Peace Sabbath/Peace Sunday. The religious communities offered a new vision and hope for a world filled with God's peace and justice.

In 1981, the United Nations General Assembly had declared that the third Tuesday of September, the opening day of the regular sessions of the General Assembly, be designated and observed as International Day of Peace. Its intent was to strengthen the ideals of peace both within and among all nations and peoples. At this time, an International Year of Peace was proclaimed for 1986.

The Sunday nearest Armistice Day (November 11) has been designated as World Peace Sunday for Protestants of the National Council of Churches. This day is devoted to prayer for peace and a world without war.

In response to the call of Jesus to be peacemakers in our time and situation, the Catholic bishops wrote a pastoral letter entitled "The Challenge of Peace: God's Promise, Our Promise." In this letter they call for the disarmament of the human heart, for a conversion of the human spirit to God, for a new vision of the world as one interdependent planet. No longer is peacemaking seen as an optional commitment but rather as a requirement of faith. The letter said, "The work of building peace has just begun. The specific strategies for making peace will be the challenge of all men and women of good will." It is to this work that the document challenges us.

Every August 6, a Peace Festival is held at the Hiroshima Peace Park in memory of the victims of the August 6, 1945, atomic bomb explosion. In 1958, a statue of a young girl, Sadako, holding a peace crane in outstretched hands, was unveiled. Children from all over the world make these paper birds and send them to Japan on this day as their prayer for peace. (Send to World Friendship Center, 1544 Mirobimachi, Hiroshima, Japan.)

Sadako Sasaki, an active student and athlete by age 12, was two years old when the atom bomb was dropped. Ten years later, Sadako died as a result of radiation sickness from the bomb. Her story is told by Eleanor Coerr in *Sadako and the Thousand Paper Cranes* (Putnam Pub Group, 1977). It is a story of love and companionship offered this young girl by family, school, friends, and the community. In her life, Sadako offers us hope, vision, and a dream when all people can one day live in peace.

A Japanese tradition states that if one folds a thousand paper cranes, one's deepest wish will come true. With courage, this little girl began to fold cranes from her hospital bed. The more discouraged she became with her illness, the more determined she was in the folding of the cranes. With each crane came the yearning to be well again and the deepened hope that war would cease. Her prayer deep in her heart was "Little crane, I write peace on your wings and send you to fly over all the world." When Sadako died in 1955, she had folded 644 paper cranes.

The remaining 356 cranes were folded by her classmates, so that 1,000 cranes were buried with her. It is these same classmates and friends that collected money from children around the world to build a statue in her honor. Across the base of this statue, the Japanese children engraved these words:

This is our cry.
This is our prayer:
peace in the world.

Peacemakers come in all shapes and sizes. We can all be signs of peace. When people come in contact with us, they should know from our presence what peace, pardon, and love are about. Together, let us build a peaceable kingdom. John Paul II used this image: "Like a cathedral, peace must be constructed patiently and with unshakable faith." A more genuinely human world is not ensured by the absence of war, but rather in living together with the full awareness of the worth and dignity of every human person and of the sacredness of all human life. We seek to construct a world of peace and justice to ensure universal respect for the human rights and human dignity of every person. As citizens of the world, we make decisions for the good of the whole human family, and show compassion for the least important in that family, the hungry, thirsty, stranger, naked, ill, the imprisoned.

Let us plant ourselves as seeds of peace and by the way we live for others, let us nourish and grow as peacemakers, instruments of God's peace. Through the peace prayer of St. Francis, we sow love, bring pardon, faith, hope, light, and joy to our troubled and broken world. "Blessed are the peacemakers, for they shall be called children of God" (Matthew 5:9).

For more information on peace activities, please write to the following groups:

Clergy and Laity Concerned
198 Broadway
New York, NY 10038

Fellowship of Reconciliation
Box 271
Nyack, NY 10960

National Council of Churches
475 Riverside Dr.
New York, NY 10115

Commission on Social Action of Union of American Hebrew Congregations
2027 Massachusetts Ave. NW
Washington, DC 20036

Pax Christi (USA)
6337 West Cornelia
Chicago, IL 60634

Sojourners
Box 29272
Washington, DC 20017

World Peacemakers
2852 Ontario Rd. NW
Washington, DC 20009

Preparations

directions

Hang the orange panel for season of fall.

Make and place the peace tree on panel.

Place four candles—representing north, south, east, and west—before the panel. (If you have a Yule Wheel, use it at this time.)

Choose a reader and a storyteller.

Choose participants to place six signs from the Peace Prayer on Peace Tree during Prayer Celebration.

Each participant should have his or her "seed name" ready for presentation.

materials

Orange panel
Four candles (Yule Wheel, if you have one)
Construction paper
Magic markers
Scissors
Pins or glue

Project

Make a tree to represent the Peace Tree and place on orange panel.

Make "seeds." Have each participant place his or her name on one of these seeds.

Divide participants into six groups. Each group is responsible for making one sign for the Peace Prayer. On the back of each sign, group members write the ways they will work to achieve peace through

Love	(a heart)
Pardon	(a hand)
Faith	(a Chi-Rho)
Hope	(an anchor)
Light	(a candle)
Joy	(a smiling face)

Make a paper crane. (If you are sending cranes to Japan, then make agreed-upon number.)

Hope

Pardon

Joy

Faith

Love

Light

Peace Tree

Prayer Celebration

Opening Greeting

LEADER: Peace be with you.

ALL: And also with you.

LEADER: May the peace of Christ reign in your hearts.

ALL: And also in your heart.

LEADER: God's work is peace. As members of one body, we are called to plant seeds of peace and to nourish their growth by the way we live for others. We light our candles of peace. To God belongs the north,

(Light candle.)

the south,

(Light candle.)

the east,

(Light candle.)

the west.

(Light candle.)

Wherever we turn to pray, there is the face of God. May these lights of peace shine in the hearts of all God's peacemakers. As God's children we become the seeds of peace. We place our seed name below our tree of peace as a sign of our willingness to grow in peace.

(pause)

Blessed are the peacemakers for they shall be called children of God.

Matthew 5:9

ALL: Blessed are the peacemakers for they shall be called children of God.

The Word of God

LEADER: The words of Isaiah ask us to become a garden with a bubbling spring of water that never goes dry as we share and nourish others in peace.

READER 1: "Remove the chains of oppression and the yoke of injustice, and let the oppressed go free. Share your food with the hungry and open your homes to the homeless poor. Give clothes to those who have nothing to wear, and do not refuse to help your own relatives. Then my favor will shine on you like the morning sun and your wounds will be quickly healed. The darkness around you will turn to the brightness of noon. And I will always guide you and satisfy you with good things. I will keep you strong and well. You will be like a garden that has plenty of water, like a spring of water that never goes dry. Your people will rebuild what has long been in ruins. You will be known as the people who restored the ruined houses."

Isaiah 58:6–8, 10–12 (adapted)

This is the Word of the Lord.

ALL: Thanks be to God.

LEADER: Blessed are the peacemakers, for they shall be called children of God.

ALL: Blessed are the peacemakers, for they shall be called children of God.

Peace Prayer and Story

LEADER: Eight hundred years ago, Francis of Assisi wrote this prayer of peace. As instruments of God's peace, we become peacemakers of our world. Lord, make me an instrument of your peace, where there is hatred, let me sow love.

ALL: Where there is hatred, let me sow love.

LEADER: As we think of ways to rid our own hearts of bitterness, we place a sign of love on our Peace Tree.

(pause)

Where there is injury, let me bring pardon.

ALL: Where there is injury, let me bring pardon.

LEADER: As we think of ways to forgive ourselves and others, we place a sign of pardon on our Peace Tree.

(pause)

Where there is doubt, let me bring faith.

ALL: Where there is doubt, let me bring faith.

LEADER: As we think of ways to relieve doubt in ourselves and others, let us place a sign of faith on our Peace Tree.

(pause and do so)

Where there is despair, let me bring hope.

ALL: Where there is despair, let me bring hope.

LEADER: As we think of ways to dispel loneliness and fear, let us place a sign of hope on our Peace Tree.

(pause)

Where there is darkness, let me bring light.

ALL: Where there is darkness, let me bring light.

LEADER: As we think of ways to brush away gloom, let us place a sign of light on our Peace Tree.

(pause)

Where there is sadness, let me bring joy.

ALL: Where there is sadness, let me bring joy.

LEADER: As we think of ways to lift the hearts and spirits of ourselves and others, let us place a sign of joy on our Peace Tree.

(pause)

O, God, grant that we may never seek to be consoled as to console,

ALL: To be consoled as to console

LEADER: to be understood as to understand,

ALL: to be understood as to understand

LEADER: to be loved as to love

ALL: to be loved as to love

LEADER: For it is in giving that we receive,

ALL: For it is in giving that we receive,

LEADER: it is in pardoning that we are pardoned,

ALL: it is in pardoning that we are pardoned,

LEADER: and it is in dying that we are born to eternal life.

ALL: and it is in dying that we are born to eternal life.

STORY-TELLER: (tells the story of Sadako and the Japanese tradition of the 1,000 cranes)

LEADER: As we place our crane on our Peace Tree in honor of Sadako and all children everywhere as they work for peace, we pray this prayer in our hearts as Sadako once did with each crane she folded:
"Little Crane, I write peace on your wings and send you to fly over all the world."

(Pause—if you are sending cranes to Japan, make your offering at this time.)

Blessed are the peacemakers for they shall be called children of God.

ALL: Blessed are the peacemakers for they shall be called children of God.

Closing Blessing: Blessing of Peace

LEADER: Peacemakers come in all shapes and sizes. We give thanks to God for calling us to do the work of peace in our world today. Bow your head for God's blessing of peace. Be a maker of peace and make gentle the ways of this world.

ALL: Amen.

LEADER: Walk in peace. Work in peace. Live in Peace.

ALL: Amen.

LEADER: Be with another in peace. Be with yourself in peace.

ALL: Amen

LEADER: Be active as peace is active, in doing something
in making something
in becoming one with God and one
with all the people God has made

(Ikonographics, *Peace,* a Reflection Film)

ALL: Amen.

LEADER: In the words of Jesus, let us offer one another a blessing and sign of peace. Let us turn to each other and say, "My friend, I give you my peace."

ALL: "My friend, I give you my peace."

John 14:27

(Offer a sign of peace.)

St. Lucy's Day

A Background Reflection

The shortest day and longest night of the year, the winter solstice (approximately December 21), was for early people a time of celebration. The winter solstice (a word from Latin meaning "sun stands still") occurs when the sun appears to be at its lowest point in the sky and appears to stand still for several days. Although this solstice marks the beginning of winter, it is also the turning point when days would begin to grow longer and warmer, nights shorter, and spring would soon return.

Ancient winter solstice festivals held in most of the northern world honored the sun and drove away winter demons with bonfires and flaming candles. The Jewish Festival of Lights, Chanukah, celebrates and marks this season and the importance of celebrating light found its way into our Christian winter festival of Christmas.

It is said that Lucy (Lucia), a young girl who live in Sicily about 300 A.D. was blinded and then killed because she would not give up her Christian beliefs. According to the old calendar, the day of her death was the winter solstice. Because of this and because her name means "light," her day became an important holiday for the Scandinavian people, where winter festivals were annually held to greet the lengthening of days and the return of light.

It was the custom for the eldest daughter in the family to dress as St. Lucy in a white gown, red sash, and wear a crown of green leaves and candles. She awakened each member of her family from sleep with coffee and cake. Her sisters would then join her and together, carrying candles and small cakes called "Lucy's buns," would travel from home to home in their neighborhood. To each home they brought a little of the warmth and light that was soon to come into the world. As a light bringer, Lucy's light was seen as a reflection of the greater light of the world, Jesus.

Customs regarding Lucy grew in popularity as "Lucy candles" were lighted in homes and "Lucy fires" burned in the open to brighten these darkest days. Into these fires was thrown incense as a protection against disease and fire.

The circle of her crown of lights was imitated by young men and women as they carried light and circled fields and orchards in a rhythmic dance step. The circle ritual was thought to turn away the demons that roamed on Halloween, Midsummer, and the winter solstice.

Houses were decorated during the winter solstice with holly, a tree honored by the ancients because it remained green all winter and even bore red berries. Popular also were evergreens, ivy, and mistletoe, which remained green through winter and thus represented strength and life. Mistletoe was honored as a sign of friendship and peace since it grew on and took nourishment from oak trees without harming them. In some northern countries it was believed that if enemies stood under mistletoe they would become friends.

The custom of lighting a Yule candle to begin the festivals of Yuletide, Christmas time, began during the Middle Ages and their celebration of the solstice. This ceremonial Yule light was also lit before all meals. This Yule candle was usually fashioned throughout the year with multiple colors of wax, always including a fragment from the year's previous Yule candle. Sometimes twelve tapers, representing the months of the year, were bound together and lit. Usually, the Yule candle base was surrounded by holly arranged in leaves of twelve. Twelve ornaments were pinned on the candle. In the lighting of the Yule candle, the prayer extended was to call on the ancients to be present at that gathering. Our Christ candle today reminds us of this Yule candle and speaks of our yearning for light during these winter months.

We need to get in touch with the moods and feelings that darkness brings to us and to experience a commonality with all people everywhere and from all times who shared similar feelings. As the sun's warmth increases till springtime, one begins to experience a triumph of light over darkness. For Christians, Jesus — as the Light of the World and celebrated as this light at Christmas — represents the same victory for all of us.

Preparations

directions

Hang the blue panel for the season of winter.

Place one large candle before the panel.
If using the Yule Wheel, place a candle on it.
Arrange seven candles in a circle around a large candle.

Place holly leaves with blessing around circle of candles. Participants will be taking these home.

Hang mistletoe.

Have names of participants for calling.

Pin paper candles to blue panel.

Choose eight readers.

Choose someone to play Lucy.

Be prepared to tell the story of Lucy.

materials

Blue panel
Candles
Holly leaves
Mistletoe
Yellow construction paper
Scissors
Pens/pencils/magic markers
Pins
White gown, red sash, greens

Project

Make holly leaves from paper or get some from florist or woods. If you use paper ones, write the home blessing on each. If you use real ones, write the home blessing on paper and tie it to each leaf.

Make paper candles from the pattern shown here. Each participant lists on his or her candle the way to bring warmth and light to others.

Dress someone as Lucia—white gown, red sash, crown of green leaves.

Prayer Celebration

Opening Greeting

LEADER: Welcome to the season of the winter solstice. We mark the time when days will become longer and the sun warmer. Sometimes darkness frightens us and we say, "Lord, give us light."

ALL: Lord, give us light.

LEADER: Sometimes darkness makes us lonely and we say, "Lord, give us light."

ALL: Lord, give us light.

LEADER: Sometimes darkness makes us confused and we do not know where to go or what to do and we say, "Lord, give us light."

ALL: Lord, give us light.

LEADER: Out of the darkness of winter nights, Jesus comes into our life as light. As we kindle the flame of our Yule candle, our Christ candle, we remember the words of Jesus:
"I am the Light of the World. No followers of mine shall ever walk in darkness. No, they shall possess the light of life."

John 8:12

(Light candle.)

Welcome Jesus as light into your heart. Out of darkness, become lighthearted in his love.

Rite of Light

LEADER: From the light of Christ, we enkindle our circle of candles.

READER 1: "You are my lamp, O, Lord. You brighten the darkness about me."

2 Samuel 22:29 (adapted)

I light this candle for my family. May they always walk in the light.

(pause)

READER 2: "Your kindness, Lord, reaches to heaven;
Your faithfulness to the clouds. In your light we see light."

Psalm 36:6, 9 (adapted)

I light this candle for my family. May they always walk in the light.

(pause)

READER 3: "God spread a cloud to cover them and fire to give them light by night."

Psalm 105:39 (adapted)

I light this candle for my family. May they always walk in the light.

(pause)

READER 4: "The Lord is my light and my salvation.
Whom shall I fear?
The Lord is my life's refuge; of whom should I be afraid?"

Psalm 27:1 (adapted)

I light this candle for my family. May they always walk in the light.

(pause)

READER 5: "God dawns through the darkness, a light for the upright; God is gracious and merciful and just."

Psalm 112:4 (adapted)

I light this candle for my family. May they always walk in the light.

(pause)

READER 6: "Your Word, Lord, is a lamp to my feet, a light to my path."

Psalm 119:105 (adapted)

I light this candle for my family. May they always walk in the light.

(pause)

READER 7: "Lord, you are a lamp shining in a dark place. We keep our eye on you until the first streaks of dawn appear and the morning star rises in your heart."

2 Peter 1:19 (adapted)

I light this candle for my family. May they always walk in the light.

(pause)

LEADER: From the circle of light we listen to the story of Lucia, St. Lucy.

(Tell story of Lucy.)

Around this crown of light we give thanks for all the people in our life who bring warmth and light to others— mothers, fathers, sisters, brothers, grandparents, relatives, friends—

(pause for spontaneous sharing or for quiet in the heart)

We have placed on our winter panel signs of the way we can bring warmth and light to others. We invite you to share what you have placed there.

(pause)

Let us form a circle around our candles

(pause)

and now listen to our call from scripture to be light bringers, to be a reflection of Jesus, the Light of the World.

READER 8: "You are not in the dark, brothers and sisters, that the day should catch you off guard. No, all of you are children of light and of the day. You belong neither to darkness nor to night. We who live by day must be alert and put on faith and love, for we are children of the light.

ALL: We are children of the light.

LEADER: We comfort and upbuild one another, for we are children of the light.

ALL: We are children of the light.

LEADER: We remain at peace and are patient toward all, for we are children of the light.

ALL: We are children of the light.

LEADER: We cheer the fainthearted and support the weak, for we are children of the light.

ALL: We are children of the light.

LEADER: We seek one another's good. We rejoice in the other's goodness, for we are children of the light.

ALL: We are children of the light.

LEADER: We pray and render constant thanks, for we are children of the light.

ALL: We are children of the light."

1 Thessalonians 5:5, 6, 8, 11, 13–18 (adapted)

This is the Word of the Lord.

ALL: Thanks be to God.

The Holly House Blessing

LEADER: It was the custom to decorate and bless the home with evergreens during the time of winter solstice. From the circle of light, we receive a holly leaf. The holly plant blooms throughout winter and becomes our sign of strength and life as we live these winter days together.
_____(Name)_____, receive this holly leaf. Place in your home (or room) as a sign of God's life and strength. Lord, bless our homes (or room).

ALL: Lord, bless our homes (or room).

LEADER: May your peace and joy abide there.

ALL: May your peace and joy abide there.

LEADER: May your goodness and mercy live there.

ALL: May your goodness and mercy live there.

LEADER: May your calm light of patience and courage shine there.

ALL: May your calm light of patience and courage shine there.

LEADER: And into our homes, may we always welcome you and all your people in a spirit of love and hospitality, we ask this in your name, Lord, as the light of our home life.

ALL: Amen.

Closing Rite of Friendship

LEADER: As children of the light we walk in friendship with each other. Mistletoe was once honored as a sign of friendship and peace. We walk under our mistletoe and offer a sign of peace by placing our hand on the shoulder of our partner.

PARTICIPANT: Peace be with you.

PARTICIPANT: And also with you.

LEADER: And now we go forth in peace and as children of the light. Together, we wait for the coming of Jesus as light in our hearts. In the light of God the Father, and of the Son, and of the Holy Spirit, live in light.

ALL: Amen.